To Andrew,
I hope you
enjoy this!
Thanks & Best Wishes
Arthur Conlin
"July 2001"

DEDICATION

In loving memory of Joan Cashin,

whose charm, grace and courage were

an inspiration to all.

A VIEW OF WALL STREET
FROM THE SEVENTH FLOOR

PREPARED AND SERVED BY THE
STOCK EXCHANGE LUNCHEON CLUB

Arthur D. Cashin, Jr.

GREENWICH PUBLISHING GROUP, INC.
LYME, CONNECTICUT

Printed and bound in the United States of America. No part
of this publication may be reproduced or transmitted in any
form or by any means, electronic or mechanical, including
photocopying, recording or any information storage and
retrieval system now known or to be invented, without per-
mission in writing from The Stock Exchange Luncheon Club,
11 Wall Street, New York, NY 10005, except by a reviewer
who wishes to quote brief passages in connection with a
review written for inclusion in a magazine, newspaper or
broadcast.

Produced and published by
Greenwich Publishing Group, Inc., Lyme, Connecticut

Design by Clare Cunningham Graphic Design
Essex, Connecticut

Separation & film assembly by Scan Communications, Inc.

Photos courtesy of The Stock Exchange Luncheon Club:
3, 4-5, 6, 8-9, 14, 18, 20-21, 22-23, 25, 26-26, 30, 32, 35,
36-37, 38-39, 40, 42 (right), 44-45, 46, 49, 53, 59, 67, 68,
74, 77, 86, 89, 90, 91, 92 and 94.

Photos courtesy of the New York Stock Exchange Archives:
31, 34 (left), 48, 51, 55, 57, 63, 66, 70, 75, 79 and 82.

Photos courtesy of CORBIS: 10, 11, 15, 16-17, 19, 29,
33, 34, 41, 42, 43, 47, 58, 69, 72 and 80.

Photo courtesy of the Connecticut River Museum, 27.

Library of Congress Catalog Card Number: 99-68224

ISBN: 0-944641-39-3

First Printing: December 1999

10 9 8 7 6 5 4 3 2

ACKNOWLEDGEMENTS

We the Board of Directors of the Stock Exchange
Luncheon Club would like to express our appreciation
and indebtedness to Arthur Cashin for his yeoman's
effort to write the witty and informative text for this
magnificent book. We would also like to express our
sincere thanks to Greenwich Publishing and Clare
Cunningham for producing this book so quickly, and
to Bill Jessup, Lauren Haines and Jodi Berman for
their organizational skills and support, to Judi
Bartolomeo for her overall coordination of the text, to
Dan Corcoran for special research, to Steve Wheeler,
NYSE Archives, to photographers Mel Nudelman
and Harry Krause for their work, and to President
Jack Dalessandro for his never-ending support and
encouragement.

IMAGE ON PREVIOUS PAGES: NEW YORK FROM BROOKLYN HEIGHTS, 1837

On June 4, 1898, "The Luncheon Club" was organized and occupied two upper stories of 70 Broadway. On June 4, 1999, "The Stock Exchange Luncheon Club" completed its 100th year with its original mission and by-laws mostly intact. Located since 1903 at 11 Wall Street, on the seventh floor of the New York Stock Exchange, the survival of the Club through wars, crashes and heady times is a testament to its past leaders and membership. As we review the past 100 years, as seen in this book, we now stand poised and ready to enter into the next century. The Club is healthy today with 1,450 active members who use this wonderful facility every day. Its good-stewardship continues under the direction of dedicated members of the Board of Directors and Committee Chairs. So, in this centennial year, as we celebrate our achievements of the past, we remember all those Members who worked so hard to maintain and bring this great Club to its present stature and success, and we give our full support and best wishes to those Directors, Committee Chairs and Members who will continue to carry the torch into the future — the twenty-first century.

— Jack Dalessandro, President

The original intent of this book was to celebrate the 100 years of fine food, fine friends and financial lore that are so much a part of the history of the Stock Exchange Luncheon Club.

But as we began to research the century of official relationship between the Luncheon Club and the NYSE, it became clear that the interweaving of food and finance in Wall Street predate our official founding and may predate the birth of the Exchange itself. In fact, the combination seems to go back to the founding of New Amsterdam. While we cannot produce an original menu, we understand the sale of Manhattan Island for $24 may well have been accompanied by the hospitality of food and drink.

Researching the early days of New York City and of the New York Stock Exchange was made easier and more pleasurable by the fact that the Luncheon Club has a treasure-trove of paintings and prints depicting that history. The majority of the illustrations in this book are pictures and prints that have hung for years in the clubrooms.

For much of the text, we have adopted and expanded many of the tales that have been featured in our newsletter, the *Bull and Bear*. The result is a kind of "snapshot" history, not unlike a family album. The style is light, conversational and, perhaps, a bit irreverent. We think that's consistent with a place where friends and foes have feasted and occasionally frolicked for over a century.

We hope you will enjoy the visual history of the evolution of a sleepy seaport town into a metropolis that is universally accepted as the financial capital of the world. We are proud of the small part the Luncheon Club played in that evolution and we are thrilled to share it with you.

TABLE OF CONTENTS

A Sleepy Island Village

It is hard for us to imagine today, dwarfed by the towers of the most famous skyline in the world, but New York might very easily have become a quaint little village.

When Giovanni de Verrazano first sailed his ship, *La Dauphine*, into New York Harbor in April of 1524, he found a lush, green place teeming with lobster, oysters, clams, deer, grouse and even bear. It might have been an ideal spot to open a quality restaurant or even for founding a settlement. Verrazano, in the employ of France, was seeking a passage to China. When he discovered that the great river he had found yielded beautiful and spectacular views of the Palisades but not a northwest passage to the Orient, he turned his ship around and sailed out. Ironically, in doing so, he sailed through the channel that would, four and a half centuries later, be spanned by a bridge that bears his name.

In his report to his sponsors, he noted that he also found unusual-looking people — "clad with feathers…of diverse colors" (little seems to have changed in New York).

New York's harbor was barely disturbed by Europeans for the next 85 years.

Then, along came Henry Hudson.

Hudson, who had been hired by the Dutch, was also looking for a passage to the Orient. He determined to explore the river that now bears his name and sailed it as far north as Albany. Sensing that the river might not lead to China, he too turned around and headed home. But not before he made note of the marvelous harbor and river he had found and the trading opportunities it held.

(Hudson did report one negative. While most of the natives whom he met were friendly, one small group was not. They killed one of the crew, a man named John Coleman…a name that would return to Wall Street and New York centuries later.)

Hudson's reports sparked great interest in Holland. So, in 1624, under the command of Captain Cornelis Mey, 30 families arrived to settle in "New Nederland." Mey's ambitions for his domain would spread beyond New York Harbor. In fact, what we now call Delaware Bay was thought to be an extension of the Atlantic Ocean. That would make the southern tip of New Jersey a "cape" (as in Cape Horn or Cape Hatteras). But this would be Mey's Cape or, as we now call it, Cape May.

NEW YORK BAY AS SEEN FROM BAY RIDGE, LONG ISLAND.

Within a year, Mey was succeeded by Willem Verhulst, who helped found the settlement of Niew Amsterdam at the tip of Manhattan. In less than a year, a ship with more settlers arrived. With them was a fellow named Peter Minuit, who would succeed Verhulst, with the title governor general of New Nederland.

Under orders from his sponsors at the Dutch West India Company, Minuit sought to arrange a peaceful purchase of the settlement area from the local natives. Minuit may have begun a 300-year tradition in New York — trying to buy wholesale. He paid a group of Native Americans the sum of 60 Dutch guilders in shiny trinkets for the whole island. (The 60 guilders is the equivalent of the legendary $24 dollars.)

Little did Peter realize that the Native Americans were starting another tradition — selling something they didn't own. Rather than being locals, the group that sold the island was a tribe from Long Island called the Canarsees. They were only in Manhattan on their way to the huge and rich oyster beds that lay where the Statue of Liberty now stands. And the chief of the Canarsees, one Seyseys, was not going to let a simple thing like not owning the property get in the way of a good sale. So he took his loot and went home — leaving Minuit to renegotiate with the Weekquaesgeeks, the tribe that really owned the joint. (Actually it was a subdivision of the Weekquaesgeek tribe called "the Manhattes.")

Since there were no bridges in New York at the time, we assume the Canarsees did not attempt another New York tradition — trying to sell one to Peter.

THE PURCHASE OF MANHATTAN BY PETER MINUIT.

PETER MINUIT

In 1632, Minuit sensed that the island needed more commerce than just trading furs with the Native Americans. So he began a great new enterprise, a commercial brewery. Soon much of the small settlement was engaged in selling or consuming alcohol.

Minuit was recalled to Holland, accused of being too liberal in ruling the area. That put the growing settlement under the guidance of a new governor general. This new top official in Niew Amsterdam lamented what he saw. His name was Willem Kieft, and he complained that he was surrounded by "grog-shops or houses where nothing is to be got but tobacco and beer" — and some food and business. Kieft's concern seemed genuine: after all, the official records of the day indicate one out of every four buildings in town had a tavern, an ale-house or a grog-shop in it.

Lest you think Kieft was a unique crank, about 20 years later, a fellow named

Peter Stuyvesant tried to rein in some fun-loving New Yorkers. Stuyvesant, whom some think could drink like a man with a wooden leg, was practical enough not to attack dining and drinking. But in January 1658, he did strike a blow for regional recti-tude. He ordered that the game of tennis not be played whenever church services were going on. (Too many McEnroe-like fights with the line judge outside the

stained-glass windows perhaps?) He also banned outright the game of "Kolven" an early form of golf (too much land use, I guess, and clearly dangerous if you hooked one over the wall at Wall Street). But old Stuyvesant's most scathing comments came in the banning of a sport called "pulling the goose" (we'll not try to describe that here).

Despite such bans, New York was viewed as a more open and enlightened town than some of its neighbors to the north.

Stuyvesant actually was a very good steward. As the town began to flourish, he began to set up rules to make things safer. He quickly addressed the greatest fear of the citizenry.

While we tend to think of colonists fighting off Native Americans, cold winters and strange diseases, the colonists tended to worry more about fire. And with good cause — at least until Stuyvesant. Tired of both fires and false alarms, "Peg Leg Pete" set out some new rules. No wooden or plaster chimneys. He appointed four house inspectors to check fireplaces and chimneys and to impose fines if structure or upkeep were shoddy. He used the fines to buy hooks and ladders and leather water buckets. He used these to outfit an eight-man nightly fire patrol that Manhattanites called "The Prowlers." (We hear that prowlers continue unofficially in New York City till this day.)

We don't know if the Prowlers became unionized, but later in that same year, 1647, Stuyvesant warned the townsfolk that Niew Amsterdam was on the verge of bankruptcy, a tradition also carried on by many later mayors.

The town and commerce continued to grow and records give us a hint whence some of that growth may have come.

The local Mohawk council sent a delegation to Stuyvesant in 1656 to make a formal request that the Dutch stop selling rum to the Native Americans. The Dutch declined, but the town was growing rougher.

So in 1658, Stuyvesant set up the first police force in America. It was called the Ratalwacht, or Night Watch. There were 12 men, and the good citizens of Manhattan determined to pay these dozen brave men a healthy sum. Reports say it was 24 stuyviers per man per night (about 60 cents). But lest ye think the government of New York City (even then) was loose with public funds, ye should know there werst "performance fines." Yea, verily, if thou were caught asleep on duty, thou wouldst forfeit 12 stuyviers.

That led to another New York City tradition — arbitrage. You sign on for 24 and if caught sleeping, forfeit 12. By New York City logic, that means you can sleep on the job for half pay — *and only if they catch you*.

With peace and quiet assured (at least at night), commerce really took off. But it didn't grow without incident. First there was the "change of ownership."

In September of 1664, a flotilla of English warships under the command of Colonel Richard Nicolls surrounded Niew Amsterdam and trained 120 cannon on the stockade walls. Outmanned and outgunned, the Dutch gave up without a fight. The settlement would change its name to New York in honor of James, Duke of York, who had been awarded these lands by his brother King Charles.

While the transition was peaceful, it did disrupt things like currency. Many people resorted to using wampum, or Native American money. This heavy use of wampum offered a unique opportunity in 1666 to a man named Frederick Phillipse.

Like many of his contemporaries near Wall and Broad, Phillipse did a good deal of his trading with Native Americans. They brought in furs, skins, food and the like. It was all quite saleable either to New York City residents or, more likely, to ship to Europe. Phillipse and other traders made a good living buying from the natives and selling overseas.

There was only one problem. There was no currency exchange. Sure you could swap pounds for guilders or francs, but the Native Americans traded for wampum — mostly the deep blue shell portions of the Quahog clam and shiny stones. The traders considered them a nuisance.

But Phillipse knew the laws of supply and demand. During a seasonal lull in the fur trade, he bought up lots of "worthless wampum" for real currency. He then buried several barrels of wampum in the backyard. When the Native Americans with furs returned, few merchants had enough wampum to bid with. Too many goods (furs) chasing too little currency (wampum) caused prices to fall. (Are you listening Mr. Greenspan?)

The falling prices nearly put the Native Americans on the warpath and most of the traders out of business. That is, until folks noticed that Phillipse had the uncanny ability to come up with just enough wampum to buy most of the now bargain-basement furs. They followed him home one night and discovered just how he could "dig up some extra cash" (wampum). He was jailed just before some Native Americans got a chance to show him a new haircut.

Nonetheless, Phillipse may have caused another first for New York — the first American recession. Over the next 30 years, New York began to really grow, despite a few wars and being recaptured by the Dutch a few times.

The Inside View of the Royal Exchange at LONDON   Vue du dedans de la Bourse Royale à LONDRES

As 1700 approached, New York experienced another key first — its first world-famous celebrity. The year was 1695, and everyone in the city was excited by the news that King William had enlisted one of New York's most prominent citizens for a special and dangerous task.

The man involved was a pillar of the community. He had an impressive house on Hanover Square and was a key part of the funding of Trinity Church. And he was not aloof or standoffish; he spoke to everyone. And everyone spoke to him, although most respectfully addressed him as Captain William because his seamanship and trading ability had brought him both wealth and fame. It is even suggested that when he left his house to begin the king's mission, nearly

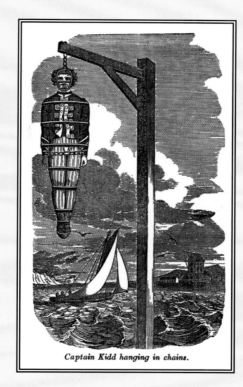

Captain Kidd hanging in chains.

half the city of New York turned out to cheer him and walk with him to his ship.

Unfortunately, when he returned four years later, it was not to cheers but to jeers. It wasn't that he didn't do his job, it was that he may have done it too well — or at least too freely. Captain William had been sent to harass and seize Spanish and French shipping vessels in the Caribbean and Atlantic. Reports were that he seized any ship he saw, regardless of its flag — British included.

So when Captain William Kidd returned to New York in 1699, he was arrested for piracy, shipped to London and promptly hung. Captain Kidd's former neighbors in New York were sure he had stashed his booty, maybe even in New York Harbor.

But Capt. Kidd did prove that you could go from hero to villain in a New York minute.

WHERE DO YOU GO TO
RENT THE SHOES?

Meanwhile, New York City continued to prosper and to grow. The city fathers thought it was prosperous enough to take on a little culture — and they could kill two birds with one stone.

The former Farmers Market, or "Markveldt," that had stood at the foot of Broadway had become an abandoned, seedy and swampy lot. A group of prominent citizens with some now-famous names like DeLancey, Chambers, Bayard, Jay and Van Cortlandt arranged to lease the lot from the city for the fabulous sum of "one peppercorn per year."

These industrious neighbors turned the swampy lot into a little park, a lovely green for "ninepins." Thus, Bowling Green became a cultural hub and meeting place for the elite of the infant metropolis.

The Bowling Green was a cultural feature of New York life for nearly a century and would become a hot spot of rebellion as the Revolution broke out.

BOWLING GREEN, 1830

HE CAN'T SAY THAT, CAN HE?

Rebellion was in the air even then (1734). Maybe not in Boston. Maybe not in Philadelphia. But certainly in that most disrespectful of media — the New York press.

The *New York Weekly Journal* seemed to take particular delight in taunting the royal governor of New York, a certain Bill Cosby (no relation, we assume). The *Weekly Journal*'s editor, Peter Zenger, was arrested on a warrant from the governor's executive council. (The governor had tried a grand jury, but even then they showed independence.)

The trial of Peter Zenger caught the attention of the colonies and even Europe. Could the press criticize the government? Were there limits? Zenger's lawyer, Andrew Hamilton, protested that the right of the people to know was important — and anyway Zenger's allegations were true. The court agreed. Thus, freedom of the press and freedom of speech were born in New York. Pick up a paper. You'll see it hasn't changed!

But it was business, not bowling nor baiting politicos, that was on the minds of New York as America began to bloom in the 1700s. While Boston and Philadelphia were vying to be the cultural capital of the colonies, New York was busy at its business.

ABOVE, BROADWAY FROM BOWLING GREEN, 1828. FAR RIGHT, ONE OF THE STAMPS ATTACHED
BY THE BRITISH GOVERNMENT TO GOODS SOLD IN THE AMERICAN COLONIES.

In fact, business was so much on the minds of New Yorkers that a group of them banded together in 1768 to found the first American Chamber of Commerce. The lure of business was so strong in New York that British soldiers were refusing to reenlist so they could take up some trade.

Yet business without bread would be barren (so we at the Luncheon Club presume). Enter an immigrant from the West Indies named Sam Fraunces. He was already a famous innkeeper in the Caribbean and was affectionately called "Black Sam." In 1762, he purchased the mansion of Stephen DeLancey, remodeled it into an inn and called it the "Queen's Head Tavern." It became a favorite of the cream of New York, including an interim visitor named George Washington. Thus the tavern, later known as Fraunces' Tavern, became one of the most famous eateries in the colonies.

Fraunces and Washington would become fast friends, and Fraunces' Tavern as well as the Fraunces family would figure importantly in the coming days of the soon-to-be "United States." But we're getting ahead of our story.

A REVOLUTIONARY TOWN

In the 1760s, Britain's relationship with its American colonies worsened. In 1765, the Parliament passed the "Stamp Act," which was an attempt to raise money by having the colonists purchase stamps to validate nearly everything — from marriage licenses to playing cards. When they insisted that you also needed a stamp to buy a drink, New Yorkers knew they had gone too far.

New Yorkers convened a meeting of most of the colonies at City Hall (Wall and Broad Streets). It became known as the Stamp Act Congress and protested "taxation without representation." The protests were heard, and the Stamp Act was repealed. But the road to revolution had begun.

By 1770, New Yorkers were challenging the British openly. The "Sons of Liberty" actually attacked a troop of British redcoats, sending several of the "lobsterbacks" to the hospital. The acting royal governor asked for more help.

As the inevitability of conflict and maybe even true Revolution became obvious to the British, they began to think about where it was most important to put their troops. They withdrew from Boston and Philadelphia, the two largest cities in the colonies. If the British had a hope of holding on to America, one place must be secured. That place, of course, was New York City.

That lesson was not lost on the ragtag Revolutionaries. They too knew that New York could be the place where the Revolution might be resolved in a single battle. So, General Washington brought his troops and a nation's hopes to Manhattan and dined at Fraunces' Tavern awaiting the British.

Washington's friendship with Sam Fraunces would not only keep the general in good food and good spirits, it would literally save his life.

In June of 1776, the British Navy sailed into New York Harbor with the largest invasion force in history. And why not? New York was strategic to the control of the colonies. That's why Washington was there to command its defenses. The British set up on Staten Island and readied to attack.

PASS THE PEAS, PLEASE

Meanwhile, however, the patriots faced another problem. There was a plan to assassinate Washington and perhaps cause the Revolution to collapse. The assassination attempt failed in a very New York way.

In mid-June a man named Isaac Ketcham began a long New York tradition. He plea-bargained his way out of jail by blowing the whistle on his co-conspirators. Ketcham was in jail on a counterfeiting charge, but the plot he revealed had nothing to do with that. The scheme that Ketcham revealed was the conspiracy to kill George Washington — led by none other than the commander of Washington's own bodyguard.

WALL STREET IN 1834 LOOKING EAST FROM BROADWAY TOWARDS SHIPS DOCKED IN THE EAST RIVER.

Washington was protected by an early form of the Secret Service, a crack team under the command of a charming, roguish Irishman named Thomas Hickey. Adding to his safety, Washington had a devoted housekeeper named Phoebe, who was the daughter of his friend Sam Fraunces. Add to that the fact that George could count on the then mayor of New York City, Dave Matthews.

Hickey was not your typical Irishman. For example: He liked a good drink (he was in debt to several tavern owners). He had a quick mind but couldn't resist a challenge (he had several gambling debts). He also had a glib tongue, could sing like an angel and could charm a dog off a meat wagon. Also he was easily bored, particularly by a revolution that was slow in starting.

So he applied his Celtic creativity to the area of design — with a specialization in the field of currency (folks with less soul would later call it counterfeiting).

When Washington started to catch on,

Hickey decided to kill the man he was sworn to protect. He found support from the mayor, who was really a Tory sympathizer. They engaged Fraunces daughter, Phoebe, to serve Washington a meal with poisoned peas.

Rather than kill her father's friend, she tipped off Washington, who promptly tipped the plate out the window. Outside, a couple of chickens promptly ate the poisoned peas and promptly tipped over and died. That raised Washington's suspicions, but they could only pin a counterfeiting rap on Hickey. That is, until Ketcham exposed the poisoning plot (and a "plan B" to enlist 700 Tory sympathizers in the Continental Army, who would then shoot Washington and most American troops at some key point of battle). Mayor Matthews later escaped to England. But Hickey was not so lucky. In less than a week, he was hanged — the first American soldier executed for treason.

Washington may have breathed a sigh of relief, but he had no time to relax. As July began, the British accelerated preparations for attack. In the early July heat, the tempers and tension of New Yorkers began to rise.

Soon word reached Manhattan that something important had happened in Philadelphia. A Declaration of Independence had been signed. By July 9, a post rider brought a copy of the document to Manhattan. Washington sensed a chance to build morale. He had the Declaration read aloud on the Commons (near present-day City Hall).

Unfortunately, the public reading took place near twilight and a few folks in the crowd may have just left "Happy Hour" at Ye Olde something or other. The crowd turned rowdy (or zealously patriotic, depending on your perspective). They stormed down Broadway to the Bowling Green and pulled down the statue of King George III that stood there. Legend has it that the lead in the statue was melted down to make musket balls. (Ironically, the statue, meant to honor the king, was ridiculed by New Yorkers. The sculptor had forgotten to put stirrups on and well…let's just say it didn't make Old George look macho.)

THIS DEPICTION OF THE
EVENT WAS OBVIOUSLY
HEARSAY BECAUSE THERE
WAS NO HORSE.

COMPANY'S COMING

The rebels had little time to relish their tact, however. Three days later, the British decided to try a little psychology on Washington and the New Yorkers. They did this by sailing just one of their hundred or so ships toward Manhattan. The ship was called the *Rose* and she carried 30 cannons.

Washington's forces had gun batteries covering the harbor. As the *Rose* moved forward, cannons blasted away from Red Hook (Brooklyn), Governors Island, Paulus Hook (Jersey City) and the Battery. No shot came near the *Rose*. In fact, she sailed all the way up the Hudson to Tarrytown. Worse yet, as the ship passed by Manhattan, it was noticed that the *Rose*'s officers sat on her quarterdeck sipping wine and waving like tourists. Not much terror or even fear there. The only casualties of the assault were Americans, killed when their cannon blew up on the Battery.

Washington began to worry.

During the balance of July and the first half of August, the British poured more and more reinforcements onto Staten Island. In fact, there were so many ships that one of Washington's men was said to have complained that the

harbor looked like "a forest of masts."

By August 22, the British felt strong enough to begin the effort to crush Washington and the Revolution. They sent 25,000 men across the Narrows to Gravesend Bay in Brooklyn. Here the troop split. The main body headed northwest toward the Gowanus Creek. The other troop, mostly Hessian mercenaries, headed for Flatbush. They got bogged down in what is now Prospect Park.

General Howe, the supreme British commander, determined to break the stalemate and press his advantage in manpower.

Howe sent a large force to trap the Americans by sweeping around them. The Brits headed up Kings Highway in Brooklyn. Then they switched to Jamaica Road. Camping overnight near what is today Bushwick Avenue, they decided on a ruse.

The next morning, they marched quietly from camp without striking their tents.

American observers thought they were still in camp. That allowed the Brits to march up Jamaica Road untested and seize the village of Bedford.

Now the Americans were virtually trapped at Brooklyn Heights — and by an army three times their size. The British were ready to capture Washington and crush his army, ending the Revolution. But that could wait until tomorrow.

So the British officers sipped claret and smiled, thinking of the rout to come.

There was no claret for the Americans, however. They were soaked from three days of rain and chilled by an unusual late August fog. It was the fog that would save them.

Washington ordered the troops to assemble silently. No one was to speak. Orders were whispered from officer to officer. The entire force of 10,000 men quietly moved from the heights to the edge of the East River. There, in rowboats and coal barges, they were rowed across the river to Manhattan. Tirelessly, the boatmen rowed back and forth. The last boatload left the Brooklyn shore just as the sun came up.

Howe had been outwitted and Washington had escaped. The Revolution lived. But barely!

I'll Take Manhattan

Washington and his bedraggled troops arrived in Manhattan to neither cheers nor parades. The populace sensed victory had been lost. Many had openly supported the rebels and if the British came, would be treated harshly. Hundreds packed up what they could carry and left everything else they had in search of safety.

Even as Washington awaited a British attack, his position worsened. Dysentery broke out among the troops, with nearly half unable to function. Morale was so low that one morning, 3,000 men of the Connecticut militia just picked up and went home. The Revolution was on the verge of collapse.

Congress sent Ben Franklin and John Adams to Staten Island to speak to General Howe at his headquarters in Tottenville. The general offered amnesty to all if only the Declaration of Independence were tossed aside. Franklin rejected the offer. The focus shifted back to Washington.

Washington knew Manhattan was indefensible. (Too much shoreline to protect.) He determined to virtually withdraw from Manhattan and relocate his troops at the north end of the island at a place called Harlem Heights. He left a much smaller defense force in place to avoid further panicking the already nervous populace.

WALL STREET IN 1829 LOOKING WEST TOWARDS TRINITY CHURCH.

HARBORING FEARS

Washington decided to try a little psychological warfare of his own. The huge British fleet sat in New York Harbor unchallenged and unthreatened. Washington had no ships to attack it, and his land cannon could not reach it. Then along came a Yale student named David Bushnell and his "submarine" called the *Turtle*.

The *Turtle* was round and was propelled by foot pedals and hand cranks. Sergeant Ezra Lee was the one-man crew that sailed the *Turtle* all the way across New York Harbor and up to the side of the *Eagle*, the admiral's flagship. Lee then attempted to attach a gunpowder bomb just beneath the waterline of the *Eagle*. If successful, the sinking of the flagship might demoralize the English or at least make them more ready to negotiate. Three times he tried. Three times he failed. So he turned around and paddled back to Manhattan leaving two more New York firsts: the first submarine attack and the first torpedo failure.

LEFT: NEW YORK HARBOR
AS SEEN FROM BROOKLYN
HEIGHTS. ABOVE, DAVID
BUSHNELL'S *TURTLE*. THE PLAN
WAS TO SCREW THE AUGER
(ABOVE THE OPERATOR'S HEAD)
INTO THE HULL OF THE *EAGLE*
(OR ANY ENEMY SHIP),
ATTACHING THE GUNPOWDER
KEG TO THE SHIP. HOW IT
WOULD EXPLODE AND SINK
THE SHIP IS UNKNOWN.

HOT TIME IN THE OLD TOWN

A week after the *Turtle* failed, the English generals made their move. They invaded Manhattan and did it with a force hardly ever seen before. Thousands of cannons on hundreds of ships rained shot and flame down on the island as thousands of redcoats poured ashore with regimental bands playing. Even grizzled British veterans said they had never seen such a display of force before.

Apparently, neither had the American militia, who fled their positions and ran north. Washington heard of the rout and raced from Harlem Heights to turn the tide. But the tide wouldn't turn. The fleeing soldiers ran past Washington. Before the British could run past Washington, some aides pulled him away to avoid his capture.

It seemed nothing could slow the British. But something did. It was not musket fire. It was not cannon fire. It was, instead, house fire. Suddenly, Manhattan was in flames. Over 500 buildings, including Trinity Church, were burning.

HALE! HALE! THE GANGS NOT HERE

The British thought the rebels had set the town on fire. There is some evidence they were right, but the Yankees denied it vigorously. Nonetheless, the Brits set about looking for infiltrators and arsonists. They certainly found one.

This guy was a bright young fellow from Connecticut. He had graduated from Yale University (where some schoolmates thought him a bit of a showoff at games). Nevertheless, he was a good scholar and had a real gift for the classics. He became a schoolteacher and looked to be headed for the role of solid citizen. When the American Revolution broke out, he (and five of his brothers) immediately joined the rebel cause.

He had rushed about trying to get into the battle du jour. Somehow, he always seemed to be a day late. And when Washington and his troops avoided defeat by slipping out of New York City, he was one frustrated guy.

So, when Washington asked for guys to sneak back into New York City to map the defenses, the schoolteacher was first in line.

NATHAN HALE, DEFIANT TO THE END.

And when his fellow officers asked how big a unit he would need, he said he'd go alone, in civilian clothes, using his Yale diploma to prove he was a schoolteacher.

For two days, he roamed successfully, making detailed drawings of British defenses and describing them in classic Latin to confuse anyone who questioned him. Then he bumped into his cousin, Samuel, who was working for the Tories. Sam identified him as Nathan Hale, a rebel spy. Hale was so proud, he said, "Yup, that's who I am!" (or the Yale equivalent).

So, on September 22, with the city still smoldering, the Brits hanged him. The rebels remembered his last words as, "I only regret that I have but one life to give for my country." It made him a martyr and a hero.

Revisionist scholars would claim that what he said was, "It is the duty of every soldier to obey his commander."

But given Hale's classic education, it is likely that he used the first version as a paraphrase of "Cato" (and today his statue stands in City Hall Park).

Washington's evacuation of Harlem Heights marked the end of New York's involvement in the Revolutionary War. The British would maintain control of the city throughout the war, and it became the refuge of many Tory sympathizers fleeing Rebels in their own states. That is not to say that the city itself was sympathetic to the British cause. In fact, when the English and their Tory pals finally left, that day, November 25, was called Evacuation Day and was both a public and official holiday celebrated grandly into the early 1900s.

Washington would not return to Manhattan for seven years. When he did return, it was only to bid farewell to his officers in the "Long Room" of the tavern that belonged to his old friend Sam Fraunces. Washington didn't know it at the time, but he would be called back to New York again in just a few years, this time to be sworn in as President of the newly won "United States."

In the spring of 1789, New York City became the new nation's first capital. New York City had already been functioning as the temporary capital under the Articles of Confederation. The Articles of Confederation, however, had proved too cumbersome and were replaced by the Constitution.

So, on March 4, 1789, the Congress of the United States would meet for the first time ever at the corner of Wall and Broad, at the present site of the Subtreasury Building. It wasn't exactly a packed house, however. Only 9 of the 22 senators showed up. The House of Representatives saw only 13 of 59 in attendance. Neither house would even get a quorum until a month later.

By the end of April, George Washington arrived and was sworn in on the balcony at Broad and Wall. Washington turned down suggestions that he wear ceremonial robes or at least his General's uniform. He wore an American-made worsted suit and silk stockings. As a concession, perhaps, he wore the dress sword he had carried through the early, dark days of the Revolution as he had scrambled fruitlessly to hold New York. After the ceremony, he walked over to the president's

BROAD STREET LOOKING TOWARDS WALL STREET AND FEDERAL HALL, 1789. GEORGE WASHINGTON WAS SWORN IN ON THE BALCONY. RIGHT, PIECES OF EIGHT.

house at Number 3 Cherry Street.

With the new Supreme Court, both houses of Congress and the New York state legislature all meeting in that same building at Broad and Wall, things began to get a little crowded. Washington had to rent space for things like the Treasury Department, the State Department and the War Department. Where did he rent? Why Fraunces Tavern, of course.

Meanwhile, signs began to show of a fatal rivalry. Alexander Hamilton would set up the Bank of New York. He also arranged for New York to limit the licensing of other banks. This frustrated Aaron Burr, who proceeded to set up a water company called the Manhattan Company in response. The company was chartered to provide water, but through a rather strange clause, was permitted to use excess funds in any appropriate manner. If you wonder what the appropriate manner was — you shouldn't — unless you've never heard of the Chase *Manhattan* Bank.

The new government of the United States faced many obstacles, but one of the key challenges was the currency — actually the value of the currency. The Continental Congress and the cooperating states had paid for the Revolution by issuing scrip, or debt certificates. The federal portion of this issuance was called "continentals."

Over the course of the war, and even after the victory, folks who had sold grain or animals or wagons to the rebels in exchange for "continentals" doubted they would ever get even. Continentals slipped to a value of under five cents to the dollar. That's when the phrase "not worth a continental" became a symbol for worthless.

Desperate for a currency for trade, many of the post-colonists began to settle deals with a Spanish coin called "the thaler," which was a kind of "piece of eight," since it was milled somewhat like sliced pizza (eight slices). Thus, you could break the coin for a smaller purchase. The "thaler" was pronounced "tholler" or "dollar," giving a new name for a future currency. Each "bit" or pizza slice was worth one-eighth of a dollar and "two bits" was worth a "quarter."

Meanwhile, Alexander Hamilton was appointed the first U. S. Treasury secretary and determined that to avoid collapse (financially), the U.S. should pay its debts, including the "continental."

Paying off the continentals would mean sudden riches to anyone who had purchased them at five cents on the dollar. There was not yet a telegraph, so how would word get to the merchants and farmers inland? Several Congressmen rented and outfitted boats to sail up rivers to places where folks had not yet heard of the planned redemption. Once on site, agents for these congressmen bought up continentals at 10 cents on the dollar (no sense being greedy!) and failed to mention the proposed redemption.

Now with several congressmen and other officials ready to make a killing, all they needed was to pass the Hamilton plan. But the plan was a few votes short. Some of the states felt it was a double hit — they had already paid off their debt and now would be taxed to pay the debt of the federal government and the other states.

Enter Thomas Jefferson. Hamilton and Jefferson usually could not agree on whether the sun was up or not. But Jefferson was homesick and felt New York had a problem — commuting, particularly from Virginia. So he swapped votes on the Hamilton plan for votes to move the nation's capital from New York to a place on the Potomac. (We won't deal with the rumors about who may have owned the property.)

To get the money to repay the continentals, the government had to issue bonds — called "publick stock." Soon many in New York were dealing in this publick stock. One of the key players was William Duer, who had been a high official in the U. S. Treasury.

William Duer was a member of the Continental Congress. He had been a signer of the Articles of Confederation. When he was married, George Washington gave the bride away. He was wealthy and getting wealthier as he traded with uncanny (and some thought unnatural) accuracy. Then charges were brought that he had performed improperly at Treasury. His empire collapsed, wiping him out and nearly collapsing the bond trading in New York. That was in March 1792.

VINCENT MARAGLIOTTI PAINTED HIS DEPICTION OF THE SIGNING
OF THE BUTTONWOOD AGREEMENT IN 1949.

The Duer collapse threatened many aspects of the New York economy, particularly because it fostered distrust. Something had to be done.

On May 17, 1792, a group of 24 merchants gathered in front of a coffeehouse at what is now 68 Wall Street. They drew up a compact that encouraged them to trade with each other. This addressed the issue of distrust squarely, by fostering trading between people who knew and could be sure of the others.

The compact was signed at a table that stood under a buttonwood tree (a form of sycamore). The agreement was immediately dubbed the Buttonwood Agreement. Decades later, when the buttonwood was blown over in a storm, newspapers carried eulogies to the great tree that had watched over a great moment.

Within two years, the merchants moved their dealing to the Tontine Coffee House. In addition to the "publick stock" there were trading opportunities in bonds of foreign nations (we were all immigrants, you know). Also canals and private turnpikes were becoming popular following the success of the Lancaster Pike between Philadelphia and the Amish farmlands of Lancaster, Pennsylvania.

Trading hours and format stayed somewhat informal until 1817, when the Exchange re-formed itself as the New York Stock and Exchange Board. Membership on the Exchange was not yet transferable, but a call market would soon be set up. Members would sit at their assigned "seats" and rise when any issue they wished to do business in was called ("Erie Canal, gentlemen! Who has business in Erie Canal?")

From its earliest days to well past its 200th birthday the NYSE traded in eighths (fractions that were one-eighth of a dollar). It all began back with the "bits" in the Spanish thaler.

Lest you think that life for these brokers was opulent, please note that records show that a common lunch was a "wedge of salted codfish and a double jigger of dark rum." Perhaps that's because there was no Stock Exchange Luncheon Club at the time. Imagine…salted cod wedges!

In late October of 1825, America completed an enterprise that would make even Ross Perot blush. When it was first proposed, nearly every government official who looked at it said it couldn't be done, and even if it could, it would be a waste of millions of dollars when the country was already carrying a huge debt. No less a figure than Thomas Jefferson had called it "sheer madness" when it had been proposed just eight years earlier.

And on paper, it surely looked like madness. Nothing like it had even been built before. To build it would require tools not even invented yet. And its structure needed material that science said couldn't be developed (like cement that could be poured and cured under 4 feet of water).

The sitting federal government urged a "no vote" on the project, saying the money was needed for higher priorities like defense. States that were not involved in the project argued that no federal funds should be used. Nonetheless, the project proceeded.

So with improper tools, improper material, borrowed money and project directors who had no skills at building anything

A PEACEFUL SCENE ON THE ERIE CANAL

similar, the builders set to work. They built a miracle through nearly 400 miles of mountains, swamps and wilderness forest. They even fought off malaria by having workers wear smoking "cat tails" on their clothes. (An interesting solution, since it would be some 80 years before science connected malaria with mosquitoes.)

The result was the Erie Canal, one of America's most successful enterprises. It made NYC a major trading hub. It helped make the nation an economic power and

sped the development of the Midwest. And about that staggering cost — well, it was $7 million, but the canal was so successful, the bondholders were paid back in just 11 years. So much for collective wisdom — particularly at the government level.

The Erie Canal success also helped the growth of the NYSE by inspiring faith in America's growth potential among foreign investors.

I Don't Mean To Be Forward, Ma'am, But I Think Your Hat Is On Fire

In the mid-summer of 1831, America began a great adventure. The Mohawk and Hudson Railroad, newly listed on the Stock Exchange, launched service on its route between Albany and Schenectady, New York.

The first train was pulled by the *DeWitt Clinton* and the passenger cars were a cross between a stagecoach and a multi-seat golf cart. Naturally, there were no windows so that folks might better enjoy the scenery and the fresh air.

The scenery in that portion of the Hudson Valley is, indeed, quite lovely. But the passengers got to see little of it. To assure that the *DeWitt Clinton* had the power to pull the loaded train over the mountainous region, the engineer and fireman heavily stoked its blazing firebox. That provided plenty of power and plenty of heavy, hot, black smoke that poured out of the smokestack and directly into the passenger cars.

Not only couldn't the passengers see, most of them couldn't breathe. And as the crew stoked the engine more, the fire became hotter but burned less completely. Hot ashes flew from the smokestack, setting fire to hats and sleeves and making the passenger cars noisier than the engine. Passengers screamed and dodged and batted away flaming, flying ash in a way that would amaze a George Lucas.

Nonetheless, the passengers arrived at Schenectady singed but safe (so to speak). Everyone knew that they had seen a modern miracle. Railroads were the way of the future. Soon scores of them were listing on the NYSE, but from then on, getting burned in railroads tended to mean something else.

STOCKS AND BONDS HELPED BUILD THE NATION'S TRANS-PORTATION SYSTEM.

On September 25, 1833, yet another piece of Americana was born on the streets of New York. It was the newsboy. You know, that scrawny-looking kid in a cap standing on a corner, hawking an "extra — read all about it." His name was Barney Flaherty, a 10-year-old kid from the Lower East Side.

And as usual, necessity was the mother of invention. Less than three weeks before, Benjamin Day had founded the *New York Sun*. It sold for a penny and would become America's first popular penny newspaper. But when it was launched on September 3, it hardly seemed a success. So on the second day, Mr. Day put an ad in his own paper. It

WALL STREET IN 1856.

read, "To those unemployed — a number of steady men can find employment by vending this paper. A liberal discount is allowed to those who buy to sell again."

A few days later, young Flaherty came upon the ad, and since it did not say, as many would in those days, "No Irish need apply," he went to see Day. After a few days of negotiating the problems (Barney had no front money and Ben needed to sell papers), they agreed to start on "trust." So on this day, Barney hit the streets, and soon he had money and Mr. Day had increased circulation. Shortly, there were newsboys everywhere.

DO I SMELL SMOKE?

Two weeks before Christmas in 1835, a terrible fire swept through downtown Manhattan (actually downtown Manhattan was still most of Manhattan).

Perhaps it was a stove, absentmindedly left "unbanked" when business was shut for the night. No one was, or is, exactly sure. All they did know was that on the night of December 16, a shop on Merchant Street burst into flames.

The fire spread quickly and ferociously. Within a few hours, several blocks and hundreds of wooden buildings were engulfed. Then, near midnight, the inferno reached the prestigious Merchants' Exchange. The grand building with its magnificent dome began to burn.

Ironically, the great rotunda was filled with supplies of some type. (Merchants met there to auction new imports.) Whatever they were, they were apparently very flammable. The heat from the rotunda fire grew so rapidly that it blew out the dome, causing a kind of chimney effect that doomed the entire building. Within an hour or so, the dome collapsed into the now-hollow skeleton of the building.

Spectators from as far away as Brooklyn and New Jersey reported seeing the awful beauty of the fiery dome imploding. All of the contents were lost — except the records of the New York Stock and Exchange Board, which had met in Room 43 of the Merchants' Exchange for several years. The records were saved by a night watchman named J. R. Mount. For his courage and quick thinking, he received the princely sum of $100.

The great fire destroyed over 700 buildings and left little but ash and embers in its wake. Luckily, it happened at night in a commercial district, so loss of property was the main casualty.

As devastating as the fire was, it burned only the southeast corner of the city. Wall Street and Broad Street were the two widest streets in the city and provided an effective firebreak. Everything between Broad Street and the East River, which was south of Wall Street, was leveled. The rest of the city was unscathed.

A new and more magnificent Merchants' Exchange was constructed in 1842. Its rotunda was so huge it could accommodate several thousand merchants.

The NYSE took up more modest quarters in the building. The Exchange ran two "call sessions" in the hall above the reading room. Eavesdroppers would call out transaction prices to the crowd in the rotunda below. The NYSE left this magnificent building in 1854. (Although remodeled somewhat, the Merchants' Exchange still stands at 55 Wall Street.)

THE MERCHANTS' EXCHANGE WAS COMPLETED IN 1842, REPLACING THE BUILDING DESTROYED IN THE 1835 CONFLAGRATION.

NEW YORK FROM WEEHAWKEN, 1819.

In July 29, 1844, the oldest yacht club in America, and one of the most prestigious clubs in the world, was founded. It was, of course, the New York Yacht Club. The founding was the result of a couple of pops aboard a small but worthy vessel called the *Gimcrack*. "We need a club," the imbibers thought. But to have a club you need a club president. Since the guy buying the drinks was the boat owner, the boys picked *him*. His name was John C. (Cox) Stevens.

When the sun came up and the glow went down, the boys realized they had somehow picked a kid from Hoboken, New Jersey, to lead this grand adventure. But your word is your bond. So they pretended they really meant it.

Stevens thought it was real and arranged with the secretary of the navy that any member of this club could skip customs upon entering any U.S. port. (What else would a Hoboken Kid ask for?) Anyway, all the "don'tcha knows" were clamoring to get on board, so to speak. And for over half a century, the New York Yacht Club was located in Hoboken at — where else — Elysian Field — where baseball happened to have been born. Talk about your cultural hubs.

FIRE AGAIN

On the 14th day of July in 1845, at about 2:30 in the morning, yet another fire broke out, this time on New Street in lower Manhattan. Since nearly all the buildings were made of wood and built butt to joist, the fire spread in a nanosecond. Then it quickly began swirling through the darkness toward the crowded docks.

Suddenly the fire engulfed one of the many "ships chandlers" shops in the teeming seaport city. This particular shop was loaded with potassium nitrate, or "saltpeter" as it was called at the time. Saltpeter was important as an ingredient of gunpowder (and it apparently served some other function among seamen).

Anyway, the raging inferno swept into the shop, igniting kegs of saltpeter. The resulting explosion rained glowing ash down on many blocks of the city.

Over the next 10 hours, virtually everyone in the city joined to fight this fire, which threatened to decimate the entire town. By early afternoon, it was finally under control, but it had destroyed over 1,000 buildings. The loss was tremendous; a cost of $10 million. (That's 1845 dollars, so today it would be billions.) The death toll was unrecorded (a bit of a tradition in NYC).

THE LATE FIRE IN DUANE STREET, NEW YORK.

BADGE OF HONOR

New York, now the fastest-growing American metropolis of the 1800s, decided to set up its own police force in 1845. And to raise their authority beyond mere uniforms, NYC gave its policemen very large, very visible copper badges (in the form of a star). So, in a xenophobic fit, the New Yorkers did not call their police "Bobbies" as the police were called in London, but rather "coppers" after the badge. Eventually it became "cops." (Some would-be linguists claim it came from C.O.P. for "Constable on Patrol" — nice try.) Later, the superior officers, like their military counterparts, would get "brass" insignia to indicate their higher rank.

NYC POLICEMAN CIRCA 1900.

THE ARTS AND ANARCHY

On May 10, 1849, a rather unique riot occurred in the city of New York. "Big Deal!" you say. "A riot in New York, how unusual!" (Well, if you can contain the sarcasm I'll explain what was unusual.)

Sure NYC has had: draft riots; race riots; religious riots; bank riots; sports riots; anti-slavery riots; and even race/religious riots. But if my research is correct, on this day (actually night) in 1849, it may have experienced its first and only acting riot.

Like most riots, the seeds had been planted long before the fighting and killing began. In this case, the planting had occurred about five years before, on a stage in London.

ABOVE: BROADWAY AT CITY HALL. RIGHT: ASTOR PLACE RIOT, 1849

By the 1840s, America was beginning to take itself seriously. It had its own poets, its own authors and even its own Shakespearean actors. Premier among the latter was a certain Edwin Forrest. Forrest was America's pride. He was considered the most accomplished actor in America.

So when he was booked to play "King Lear" in London in 1844, America felt his expected rave reviews would validate that America had finally attained cultural parity with Europe. But the reviews were anything but raves. Critics called him amateurish and saddled with American coarseness. And even before the reviews, the opening night audience had hooted and hissed Forrest nearly off the stage.

Forrest was convinced that his London tour had been sabotaged by William MacReady, England's "Premier Actor." Thus, when Mr. MacReady came to tour America in 1849, Mr. Forrest, seeking revenge, was lying in wait. He scheduled performances head-to-head against MacReady. More importantly, he rushed to give interview upon interview retelling how nasty the British had been to him, thanks to MacReady.

The campaign worked. On May 8, 1849, MacReady opened at the Astor Place Opera House. Unbeknownst to the star, the audience was packed with Forrest's friends, who were also packed with a lot of yet to be recycled fruits and vegetables. As MacReady spoke his first lines, the audience recycled the produce at MacReady. Ungratefully, MacReady fled the stage and announced he was through with America.

The "don'tcha knows" were incensed and got the mayor to offer more police and even the National Guard to protect MacReady's next performance. But all the publicity inspired even greater anti-MacReady feelings. So a crowd of 12,000 or so marched on the Opera House. (They were led by a certain E. Z. C. Judson, who would later hide his police record by changing his name to Ned Buntline, write dime novels and create Western heroes.

Anyway, on this night, the mob of 12,000 started throwing cobblestones at the theater, the cops and the troops. (Now if you have not been in a New York riot recently, let me assure you that hurled cobblestones can sting more than rubber bullets.) So the cops, lacking a sense of humor, opened fire, leaving 30 dead and 50 injured.

And so the nation's first and certainly worst theater riot ended.

IF YOU BUILD IT, THEY WILL COME

In 1851, the world press was agog with wonder at the "Great Exhibition of Industry" which had opened in London. It featured works and inventions from many nations (a precursor of a world's fair). But what drew almost as much attention as the exhibits was the place in which they were housed — the Crystal Palace of London.

It was a masterpiece of glass and cast iron that some compared to the Parthenon or the Colosseum. The building was a marvel and was said to be an example of what marked a truly global city.

Well, that was all the aspiring New York City don'tcha knows needed to hear. It's not enough that they had set up a police force like London, now they needed a Crystal Palace. So, the likes of August Belmont and William Cullen Bryant solicited the Schulyers and the Bergins and the Vander these and the Vander those.

But where shall we locate this wondrous building? The city was already densely populated. Years ago, it had spilled north of Wall Street, past Bleeker Street and then all the way to 23rd Street. Where could you put a building so large?

Belmont and his friends suggested a site nearly a mile north of the nominal north end of the city at Madison Square. The building committee suggested a spot way out in the sticks, near where the reservoir was located — in the boondocks — at 42nd Street.

Critics were quick to pounce. Build at 42nd Street? Why not the North Pole, or even New Jersey? How would folks get there? No fashionable horse-drawn busses went that far north. But the builders would not be deterred.

Amazingly, within two years, the builders had constructed a wonder of the world — at least the New World. At the junction of 42nd Street and 5th Avenue, shimmering in its own gaslights, the glass and iron wonder invited the curious and the common to walk past fountains and marble surrounded by the world's inventiveness. It seemed to have everything — telegraphs, photographs, airship designs, elevated railroads and automatic ice cream makers. (Remember…this is 1853…and these are wonders!)

The grand opening was grand indeed. President Franklin Pierce came and spoke. So did the mayor and many luminaries. It wasn't just a building. It was a symbol of a new era — prosperity, peace and creativity.

Immediately, 42nd Street did not seem so far. Bus owners made special runs, which

Designed by Carstensen & Gildemeister 74 Broadway N.Y.

New York Cryst

This building, constructed of Iron and Glass, is erected on Reservoir Square in the City of New-York, by the Association
The Ground Plan of the Building forms an octogon, and is surmounted by a Greek Cross, with a Dome over the Intersect

GEORGE J. B. CARSTENSEN & CHARLES GILDEMEISTER *Architects.*   WILLIAM WHETTEN, *Vice Pre Treasu*

EDMUND HURRY, *Consulting Architect.*   L. C. STUART, *Assistan*

ace for the **Exhibition** of the **Industry** of all **Nations.**

SON OF THE INDUSTRY OF ALL NATIONS, incorporated under an Act of the Legislature of the State of New-York, the 11th day of March, 1852. The use of Reservoir Square is granted by the Municipal Authorities of the City ...
ngth and breadth of the building are each 365 feet. Height of Dome to top of Lantern, 148 feet. Entire space on Ground Floor, 111,000 square feet. Galleries, 62,000 square feet. Whole area, 173,000 square feet or 4 acres

DIRECTORS:

MORTIMER LIVINGSTON.   ELBERT J. ANDERSON.
ALFRED PELL.   PHILIP BURROWES.
AUGUST BELMONT.   JOHNSTON LIVINGSTON.
ALEXANDER HAMILTON, Jr., CHARLES W. FOSTER.
GEORGE L. SCHUYLER.   THEODORE SEDGWICK.
WILLIAM WHETTEN.   WILLIAM W. STONE.   HENRY R. DUNHAM.

THEODORE SEDGWICK, President.

C. E. DETMOLD, Superintending Engineer.
HORATIO ALLEN, Consulting Engineer.

Lithography of Nagel & Weingärtner 74 Fulton St. N.Y.

Published by GOUPIL & Co. 289 Broadway New York.

soon became regular runs. Thousands came every day. Folks from all across America came (among them a young Mark Twain, who spoke with wonder of the wonders).

It might have lasted for a hundred years, and it should have, since its glass and iron beam construction were thought to make it fireproof. But only five years after its grand opening and in the midst of great popularity, the Crystal Palace fell victim to a fire that began in a storage room. It may have been paint. It may have been cleaning cloths. But suddenly, rather spontaneously, fire burst forth. It also burst down, unfortunately, and lit up the floor boards.

Yes, it was glass and iron, which were fireproof. But the floors were wood. Suddenly thousands of square feet of flooring were burning — burning so hot that the nearly 20,000 panes of glass melted, warping the cast iron frame. The most fabulous and beautiful building in America was no more.

There was no serious attempt to reconstruct it. Maybe even then, they knew there would be other buildings to catch attention — the Flatiron, the Chrysler, the Empire State and the World Trade Center, among others. Some might even be places even a monkey could love.

On July 14, 1863, the terrible New York draft riots began. Two days before, the government had begun America's first draft. It included all U.S. males between 21 and 45. And it included all males of that same age group who happened to be aliens intending to stay in the U.S. This included a very large number of Irish immigrants who had fled the potato famine in 1848.

Since the government at the time was not enlightened enough to provide the kind of work that these men felt they were suited for — tellers of tales, singers of songs and dreamers of dreams — the Irish tended to settle for 14-hour-a-day jobs digging sewers for less than one dollar a day. And when the draft came up, they were upset that rich men's sons bought their way out of the war (legally) by paying $300. They were even less happy that some of the jobs they were drafted away from seemed to be taken up by the newly freed slaves.

So, after a pint or two they decided to riot. (Author's Note — A bit about my fellow Irishmen. We Celts are good at wars

LOOKING EAST ON WALL STREET TOWARDS THE
SUBTREASURY, LEFT, AND THE MERCHANTS' EXCHANGE,
RIGHT (SEE PAGES 36-37).

— though we rarely win them. We are good at songs — though they make you cry. We are good at stories — though no one believes them. But riots clearly are not our strong point.)

Nonetheless, the New York Irish began three days of burning the wrong houses, lynching the wrong people and managing to get a thousand of their own killed. Inspired by all this, they decided to bring the fight to a head. Since the militia was beginning to make lower New York City no fun, they

headed north to the house of one Horace Greeley, the abolitionist editor, whose compelling editorials seemed to help incite the war.

Greeley was not home, but his wife and kids were. Mrs. Greeley saw the maddened mob and sent the kids out of the house. Then, according to some reports, she positioned herself in the doorway with a torch and a small bucket of gunpowder (okay, so maybe *you* don't keep a small bucket of gunpowder around the house but that's *you*).

Anyway, on learning Mr. Greeley was not home, these sons of Erin (and of the world's oldest matriarchal society) piped up, "Now Missus, you wouldn't be burnin' your house about a simple matter like this riot, wud ya?" Apparently, she said she would, and so the Irish mob went home to kiss their moms and to enlist in a war with drums and guns and shouting.

(Two years later, on the anniversary of that very day, perhaps fearing returning Irish veterans, Greeley wrote his famous — "Go West Young Man" editorial.)

STEPHEN COLLINS FOSTER, 1826-1864.

In early January of 1864, America lost a genius. We didn't know it at first. It all began when one of the doctors at Bellevue Hospital in NYC pulled a sheet up over the corpse of an apparently unknown homeless young man. The deceased clearly had been a drinker and was mildly tuberculous. The tag at the foot of his litter read — "Forster."

The body stayed unclaimed and was moved to the city morgue. Three more days went by, and then an old neighbor and friend came by to claim the corpse. It was only then that the hospital staff realized that the man's name had not been "Forster" but rather Foster — a certain Stephen Foster — America's first and most prolific songwriter.

His songs are so much a part of Americana that two states even adopted some as official songs — Kentucky, naturally: "My Old Kentucky Home," and Florida, ironically and prophetically: "The Old Folks at Home." But he also wrote "Oh Susanna!" "Jeannie with the Light Brown Hair" and "Camptown Races," among hundreds of others.

But in his 30s, life and health turned against him (not unlike another musical prodigy — Mozart). He became bitter and depressed, and his talent seemed to leave him. So when a fall and a resulting gash wounded him fatally, it was a blessing.

As his friend collected Foster's belongings and body, he came across a crumpled piece of paper. On it was written Foster's final and, some feel, his most beautiful song. And it may have reflected the young man's weariness with life. On the paper was written:

Beautiful dreamer, wake unto me.
Starlight and dew-drops are waiting for thee.
Sounds of the rude world heard in the day,
Lull'd by the moonlight have all pass'd away.

Foster's wonderful legacy lives with us all. But despite the joy and beauty of his songs, he was yet one more genius lost to drink and depression.

On Friday, September 24, 1869, an attempted (and nearly successful) corner in the "gold market" crumbled, sending gold and stock prices plummeting and ruining scores of brokerage firms. The devastation was so swift and so great that one of Wall Street's most prominent brokers (Solomon Mahler) was driven to commit suicide. The corner had been based on a script that could have made "Dallas" seem like "Dick and Jane go to market."

In addition, it had a villain to make J. R. Ewing look like Mother Teresa. His name was Jay Gould, and he was not just a robber baron, he may have been the baron of robbers. He had made a nickel or two (okay, millions) by a variety of enterprises like shorting the stock of his own companies. When squeezed, he simply printed more shares — or selling woolen blankets to the Union Army. (Okay, so they were frayed linen and of irregular shape and maybe not actually wool.)

Anyway, with the opportunities of war behind him and with millions burning a hole in his pocket, he decided to make some money with his old friend President Grant. Oh sure, he had never actually met Grant, but isn't a friend just someone you haven't met yet?

Thus, Gould told Wall Street that his pal Grant had decided to follow Gould's advice and inflate the currency by stopping gold sales by the Treasury. (Gould had bought gold at about $120, along with his allies.) When some cynic noted that Gould and Grant had not been seen slapping and tickling at Delmonico's recently…er…actually ever, Gould knew he needed a foil. So he offered a share in the scheme (…er, make that "plan") to the president's brother-in-law, Abel Corbin. Gould immediately embarrassed doubters by noting how often he and Corbin were "hanging out." The scheme worked well (gold rose to $162).

Then Corbin called to say Grant was irate and would soon release $4 million in Treasury gold. Needing buyers, Gould called his old partner Jim Fisk and asked him to set up phony accounts at various brokerages to create the false impression that there were buyers. Not that anyone would "front run," but suddenly there were bids, and Gould hit them all. But the brokerage firms that had taken his (Fisk's) phony buy orders had to honor those trades.

Simply put, Gould collected on the gold that he had sold to himself, but defaulted on the buy side. Thus he bailed himself out on Wall Street's back. The result was a collapse in gold, stocks, bonds and brokerages. When the news hit of Treasury sales, Gould was completely out (already having sold to his phony bids). It was a disaster that America would not shake for nearly 20 years. In your history books, it is called "Black Friday."

A CHECK FOR $5,000 WORTH OF GOLD IN 1865.

BROADWAY WITH TRINITY CHURCH IN THE BACKGROUND AS SEEN IN A MID-NINETEENTH CENTURY DRAWING.

CULTURE AT A PENNY A PACK

In December 1869, William Semple of Ohio was granted a patent on a form of chewing gum. Americans had long chewed a variation of an old Native American substance — a combination of sap and paraffin.

But like many American inventions, somewhere else another guy was working on the same project. In this case the somewhere else was Staten Island.

A guy named Santa Anna, who had a brief political and military career in Mexico (and some adventure at a place called the Alamo), was trying to start a new career in his 70s. And where is there a trendier, more intellectually challenging place to do so than Staten Island. He was hoping to produce a substitute for rubber and had brought along some chicle (itself the sap of a Mexican plant).

He showed a sample to a local inventor, Tom Adams. But try as he might, Adams couldn't make a rubber substitute. So one day, while Adams was hanging out at a drug store (the mall had not been invented yet), he heard a kid complain about the paraffin gum. Adams went home, soaked some chicle in licorice and kneaded it into little pellets. The druggist sold out the first batch in under six hours. Shortly, America was hooked on "Adams N.Y. Gum No. 1."

Thus, New York became "the" locale for gum-snapping, wise cracking guys and dolls.

THE AGE OF THE ROBBER BARONS

The man to whom the term "robber baron" was first applied began as a kid from Staten Island. Please note we did not say "simple" kid, for there was nothing simple about him. His name was Cornelius Vanderbilt, and, as we'll discuss later, he was known as "The Commodore."

As a young lad, Vanderbilt got access to a small skiff and convinced friends, family and folks in the area to let him ferry presents, products and postage to Manhattan and New Jersey. He quickly discovered he could bring goods back on the return voyage and double his profits. Soon, he was out-sailing, out-shipping, outsmarting or out-shoving his competition. In just a few years, the kid from Staten Island controlled virtually all the shipping traffic in New York Harbor.

Then Vanderbilt struck gold. Actually, it was a guy named Marshall at Sutter's Mill in California who struck real gold in 1849. But Vanderbilt knew an opportunity when he saw one. Buying up a small fleet of ships, he soon was making a fortune shipping prospective prospectors to Frisco and returning laden with Pacific products. That's when folks began to call him "Commodore" (some claim it was a

PUCK MAGAZINE DEPICTED WILLIAM VANDERBILT LOOKING DOWN THE STEPS OF THE SUBTREASURY AT JAY GOULD, SINKING IN A POOL OF WATERED STOCK.

DROWNING IN HIS OWN "POOL."

nickname sarcastically given back when he was a one-skiff kid putting on airs. Later, it seemed grudgingly deserved.)

So there he was, 66 years old and very successful — worth $11 million (about $2 billion today). Time to relax — maybe retire? Not Vanderbilt! He began looking for ways to move his goods off the dock find even more customers. He turned to the railroads, a form of transport he had previously hated and avoided since he was injured in America's first fatal train crash in 1833. Hate was one thing — profits were another.

In those days much of the beef consumed on the East Coast came from upstate New York. Vanderbilt discovered that the New York and Harlem Railroad had a terminus in Brewster, New York, a key junction for cattle drovers. Vanderbilt quietly bought majority control of the railroad at about $9 per share. When word leaked out, a short squeeze drove the price to $50. That gave Vanderbilt a taste for several things — Wall Street, buying railroads and short squeezes.

Over the next 14 years, he bought or bullied his way into railroads, rights of way and regional relationships. And when buying or bullying didn't work, history says he bought judges and occasionally whole state legislatures. Hey! When you need a favorable ruling, you *need* a favorable ruling. That's when he became known as a "robber baron."

Perhaps Vanderbilt's own words give hint of his temperament and the temper of the times. Vanderbilt sought revenge on a bad deal once by saying, "You have undertaken to cheat me. I will not sue you, for law takes too long. I will *ruin* you!"

When he died, he was the wealthiest man in America. Let's put that in perspective. Vanderbilt died in 1877 with an estate of $104 million — that was $4 million *more* than there was in the entire Treasury of the United States in that year.

Another robber baron was a man who battled and once beat Vanderbilt. He was a Wall Street villain who preached teetotaling but was an episodic drunk, yet he founded a New York area college that still bears his name.

The man in question was Daniel Drew (Drew University). "Uncle Daniel," as he was sarcastically called, was reputed to have invented or "improved" some of the meanest tricks in Wall Street. Contemporaries claimed he would sell out a partner the minute the partner was out of sight. During a vicious short squeeze, Drew was said to have originated that classic Wall Street line — "He who sells what isn't his-in; must buy it back or go to prison."

Drew started as a circus roustabout but soon became a cattle drover. He reportedly would feed the cattle a great deal of salt when they hit Brewster but not let them drink until they hit the Harlem River — thus they weighed a lot more when they arrived for weighing at the Manhattan stockyard. Drew's gimmick became known as "watered stock" and he would use a variation many times in Wall Street. His experience as a drover never left him. Many years later he remarked, "to speculate in Wall Street when you are not an insider is like buying cows by candlelight."

Maybe it was the weight of all his misdeeds that caused reports that he would "...rent a room, close all the windows, bury himself under a pile of blankets and drink until he passed out." (He probably knew that wouldn't be tolerated at the Luncheon Club.)

In September 1873, the New York Stock Exchange set a record, although it was one they would be ambivalent about for the next 108 years.

Founded in 1792, the Exchange had survived early volatility (1794), a challenge from competitors (1802), a merger and a new name (1825), a punishing diet (lunch was a double jigger of dark rum and a wedge of dried codfish, circa 1810: please note…we no longer serve codfish).

But on Saturday, September 20, 1873, for the first time in its history, the NYSE closed in response to a panic. (The term "circuit breaker" had not been invented yet…er…neither had circuits.)

A week or three before, perhaps the most renowned firm in U.S. Treasury auctions had doubt cast upon it. The firm was Jay Cooke & Company. And on most continents, it was seen as a major player. After all, its aggressive style had made it the key underwriter for the billions of Treasury bonds issued during and after the Civil War. (Contemporary critics did complain that deficit spending had gotten out of control.)

Anyway, the dent in the reputation of this key brokerage firm only confused the

THE TWICE-DAILY CALL OF STOCKS.

market at first. But as the second half of September approached, there were hints that the problems would spread to other brokers. On September 18, liquidation of equities showed up at the "first call."

In those days, the buying and selling of stocks by members of the Exchange ocurred only during the morning or afternoon "call." Listed companies were called one at a time, and any member wishing to buy or sell shares of that company rose from their assigned seat to haggle over the price. This twice-daily call of stocks was replaced in the 1870s by the continuous trading system still in operation today. But the need for each member to have his own seat had already created the imagery between a membership in the Exchange and owning a seat.

So, here we were. Rumors surfaced of other brokerage firms involved, and the first call on the 18th turned soft. The second call turned soggy. Prices were down, and with no ongoing after-market, all you could do (as the banks had to do) was await the next call.

The morning call on the 19th was even messier, and the afternoon call was just a plain disaster. By the morning of the 20th, anyone who was in the phone book (if there had been a phone book at the time) was rumored to be involved or impacted by the problem.

So, naturally the morning call on the 20th was a bigger disaster. So much so that the Exchange opted to close until the crisis calmed (completely skipping the afternoon call).

Close they did and for a lot more than one "call." But, perhaps because banks and investors naturally needed some means of evaluating holdings, they reopened about 10 days later. However, the rumors would not go away, and liquidations and defaults continued. The history books call it the Panic of 1873. And it put the American economy in a tailspin for years. (Nearly 10,000 businesses failed.)

In May 1883, the city of New York was changed by a miracle — not the heaven and angel type, but a miracle of engineering. It was called the Brooklyn Bridge, and it captured the spirit of the times and the imagination of the public.

Some, however, thought the bridge was cursed. In the very beginning of construction, the design engineer, John Roebling, had his foot crushed between a barge and a pier. The wound became infected, and tetanus developed. Roebling was dead within months.

Roebling's son, Washington, then took over management of the project. Quickly, however, the bridge would take his health too. Washington Roebling spent much time with the "groundhogs" below the surface, digging the caissons that would support the bridge towers. Like many groundhogs, he developed nitrogen narcosis, or what we laymen call "the bends." It so weakened Roebling that he was forced to direct the next 10 years of construction from an apartment overlooking the bridge site.

The Roeblings were not the only victims of the massive project. Scores and scores of workers lost life or limb in the effort.

Despite the cost in money and men

(or maybe because of it), the public was fascinated. Crowds would show up each day to watch in awe the construction of the 30-story towers or the lacing of cables or whatever was going up.

Finally, in May 1883, the Brooklyn Bridge was opened. It was deemed such a miracle that President Chester Arthur, New York Governor Grover Cleveland and scores of other dignitaries (foreign and domestic) crowded the reviewing stand so that it groaned under the weight. Fireworks, bunting and bravado to befit a wonder of the world was the order of the day. But some felt the curse still lingered.

Just five days later, the Brooklyn Bridge was returning to normal after its spectacular grand opening. Some bunting remained, but gone were President Chester Arthur and Governor Grover Cleveland and the hundreds of celebrities and officials that had surrounded them.

In their place were horsecarts and handcarts and hundreds of people transversing the "miracle span." Amidst the din of commerce, someone untrusting of the technology of the 1880s may have remarked that they had felt the bridge move or tremble or seen the cables unravel. Whatever was said,

his companion must have been hard of hearing and mumbled something like "Whad ya say?"

The comment was repeated loud enough to be heard by the companion and everyone within 50 yards. The panic that ensued resulted in 12 trampled to death and scores injured.

The mystery and myth around the bridge continued. It was rumored to be a suicide site. No one could survive the 14-story drop from the walkway to the East River below. But this is New York. Whenever you say never, someone has to try.

Along came Steve Brodie. Brodie was a bookmaker, but he was no celebrity — just a nondescript local wise guy. At least until one hot July night in 1886.

Brodie had let on to just enough people that he was planning to jump off the Brooklyn Bridge. The hint allowed for a small group of onlookers to confirm the event to press and public alike.

To the gasps of the onlookers, Brodie jumped from the bridge, disappearing into the murky river then resurfacing to swim across current to shore — and to fame.

Many New York cynics, including a few of the onlookers, doubted it was Brodie

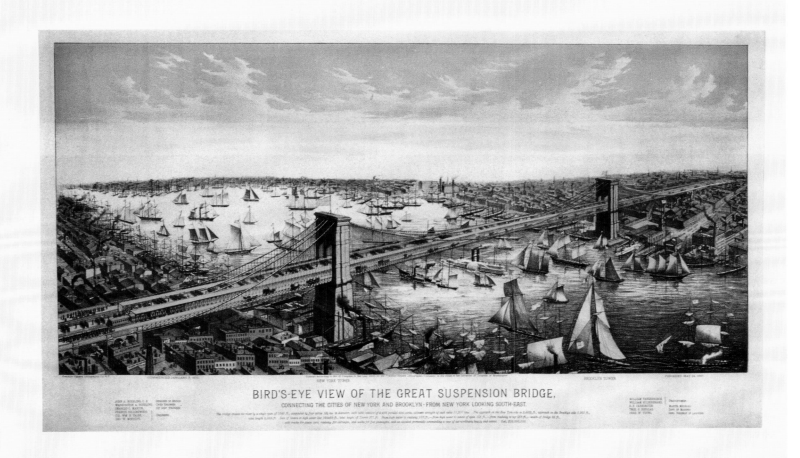

BIRD'S-EYE VIEW OF THE GREAT SUSPENSION BRIDGE.
CONNECTING THE CITIES OF NEW YORK AND BROOKLYN · FROM NEW YORK LOOKING SOUTH-EAST.

who jumped. They thought it was a dummy, dressed in identical clothes to Brodie and weighed down with stones to disappear into the river. Brodie was thought to be waiting under a strategic pier to bob up at the appropriate time and claim celebrity.

Whatever the truth, Brodie became famous, and he bought a saloon to capitalize on his celebrity. He later appeared on Broadway (often as a man destined to jump from a bridge).

Shortly, the East River was crowded with bridges, and the city of Brooklyn merged into the city of New York. Even today, some Brooklynites feel that was the worst curse of the bridge.

The journey to Brooklyn continued to inspire creative construction solutions. The Brooklyn Battery Tunnel was the longest underwater vehicular tunnel when it was built in 1950. It still is today.

SPRING WILL BE A LITTLE LATE THIS YEAR

It had been a particularly warm March day in 1888. New Yorkers poured onto the streets at lunchtime hoping to enjoy the sun and fresh air. Actually, it had been a mild winter, the mildest in two decades, according to records. The newspapers suggested that the next day, March 12, would be a bit cooler with occasional gusty winds. Talk about your understatements.

If you awakened at 6:00 a.m. and peered out your window, you would find that the "bit cooler" was 13 degrees above zero with two feet of snow already on the ground, drifting to nine feet in 50-mph winds.

That was just the beginning.

Before noon, the wind would increase to 90 mph, blowing the crosses from church steeples, snapping hundreds of telephone poles and hurling store signs along as unguided missiles. Trains and horsecars ground to a halt. On that new marvel, "the El," nearly 20,000 people were stranded in various trains at various locales. Neighborhood assistance groups sprang up, putting ladders up to the stranded cars and helping each passenger to the ground. Helping each passenger, that is, who could

pony up $1 for ransom. (In 1888, one dollar was a half week's pay for lots of folks.) If you lacked the gratuity, you could remain on the stranded train, rocking on the elevated track in 80-mph winds as snow swirled through the blown-out windows. (Moral: always carry a buck when traveling in New York.)

The New York Stock Exchange managed to open on time at 10:00 that morning, though only 61 of its 1,100 members were present. With virtually no one there and with ruptured phone lines shutting off customer contact, the Exchange closed at noon. That was not particularly good if you were a broker hoping to make it home.

After noon, the storm began to get really ugly. The storm was based offshore and ran tides up over storm walls, flooding streets and then freezing solid. Shipping, which was a primary means of transportation and commerce, was devastated. Ship after ship was smashed against piers and wrecked. There were so many blocks of ice in the East River that there was a natural "bridge to Brooklyn." Later, newspapers would report that one man nearly suffocated when his mustache froze to his beard

and he couldn't open his mouth.

The snow would continue to fall. Some later estimates said nearly four feet had fallen. The winds kept blowing at gale force, raising drifts to 20 feet (as high as a two-story building). Over 400 people froze to death on the streets — stranded en route to home or to somewhere.

Coal supplies ran out (it was supposed to be spring, after all). Furnaces shut down. Telephone and telegraph lines were torn and useless. The city was marooned, with all roads and rivers impassable and no communication possible.

But this was the age of American ingenuity (and it was New York, after all). So, police, hospitals and even stockbrokers sent messages to London via the undersea Atlantic cable. London was then able to relay the messages to Boston, Philadelphia and elsewhere. Soon help would be forthcoming. This was how they survived the Blizzard of '88. Moral: where there's a will (and an undersea cable), there's a way.

NEW STREET LOOKING NORTH TOWARD WALL STREET AFTER THE BLIZZARD OF MARCH 12, 1888.

YOU LOOK MARVELOUS

JAMES BUCHANNAN "DIAMOND JIM"
BRADY, 1856-1917.

One of the most colorful characters in American finance was certainly Diamond Jim Brady. Always flamboyant, and often flashy, Brady was fond of saying, "You've got to look like money to make money." While it is suggested that he may have come to the Stock Exchange Luncheon Club from time to time, his favorite haunts were more nocturnal — such as Harry Hill's, Delmonico's and Louis Sherry's. These were frequented by a few other notables; among them a certain Thomas Edison, a certain P. T. Barnum and a certain John L. Sullivan.

While Brady was renowned for his glittering diamonds (shirt studs, stickpins, rings, cane tops, etc.), his elegant cutaways and his constant and beautiful companion, Lillian Russell, he was even more fabled for his legendary appetite.

Incredibly, a not-unusual meal for him was: a clear soup, three dozen oysters, half a dozen crabs, several lobsters, two ducks, aspic of goose, steak, three corn on the cob, assorted vegetables, pudding, cheese, fruit, pastry and a box of chocolate. All of this was washed down with a pitcher or two of orange juice. The meal was, of course, followed with several fine cigars (in the smoking section, we presume).

The mystery of Diamond Jim's appetite was solved several years before his death. While operating on Diamond Jim, doctors discovered that his stomach was six times larger than the average man's. (Thank goodness! I was beginning to feel like an underachiever.)

When Brady died in 1917, thousands gathered to pay their respects to the man once called "the happy friend of all New Yorkers, from newsboys to nabobs."

PROPOSED ARCADE RAILWAY UNDER BROADWAY
LOOKING NORTH NEAR WALL STREET.

Aside from their love of money, Hetty Green ("the witch of Wall Street") and John D. Rockefeller shared something else in common. They both spent the latter part of their lives consuming nothing else but graham crackers. (Okay! Okay! Maybe an occasional glass of milk.)

Many Wall Streeters were devotees of graham crackers, the miracle health food of the very late 1800s. Dr. Sylvester Graham had preached clean living, reform and whole wheat for decades. Plot and Plunder by day; Piety and Powdered Wheat by night. The Gilded Age occasionally could show signs of gastronomic anxiety.

In fact, others built on Dr. Graham's concepts. One fellow who would later become famous opened a sanitarium in Michigan. Seeking some variations on graham crackers, he developed wafer-thin sheets of toasted grain bread. When one batch broke into flakes, he served them in a bowl for breakfast the next morning. All his patients loved these "corn flakes," and the gent, a man named Kellogg, knew he had a hit on his hands.

One of his patients, who ran out of money (pre HMO's), asked for a job at the sanitarium so he might pay his own way. When he was turned down, he set out to duplicate the sanitarium (with him in charge, of course). He developed a coffee-like breakfast drink and a cereal of his own. His name was C. W. Post, and his health foods were called Postum and Grape Nuts.

(Odd note — while Rockefeller lived to 98, Dr. Graham, the man who developed the lifesaving crackers, died an invalid in his 50s.)

One of the recurring themes in this history has been the inextricable link in American history of food, drink, finance and fashion. At no time was this link so pervasive as it was at the period near the turn of the century.

At that time, the captains of finance and the robber barons (sometimes interchangeable) tired of flaunting their wealth with brick and mortar (er…actually brass and marble would be more accurate). Having out-muscled each other in commerce and out-mansioned each other on Fifth Avenue and at Newport, they now began to out-entertain each other.

In 1905, for example, Mrs. Astor threw a Grand Ball shortly after New Year's Day. Only 400 people were invited, since that's all the grand ballroom at the Astor mansion could hold. (Don't scoff! How many cronies does your grand ballroom hold?)

Anyway, the limit of 400 made the list quite selective, and anybody who aspired to be somebody clamored to be invited. That's how the phrase "the 400" came to be synonymous with "high society." It was such an event, that Harry Lehr threw a pre-dinner

dinner at the St. Regis. (Just 100 close friends, each table had 3,000 roses on it…where did they put the food?) Then they all went on by hansom cab to Mrs. Astor's bungalow.

There they had canvasback duck, three kinds of fish, terrapin, foie gras and much more. They washed it all down with gallons of Krug '98 and Apollinaris water. (Pour it in the golden finger bowl, Pierre!)

After much dancing, accompanied by more Krug '98, they probably picked up the favors Mrs. Astor had provided for each guest. Each attendee received a gold pencil case, a set of leather pen wipers, a silver paperweight, a Directoire cane, a china figurine, a buggy whip, a rubber-bulb polished-brass carriage horn, a leather letter case and jardinieres. Then they sat down to four more courses and several more flutes of Krug '98.

Not to be outdone, seven weeks later, Mr. and Mrs. James Stillman threw their own grand ball…after first constructing a 25-foot waterfall in their ballroom. Then Rudy Guggenheimer threw a little soiree at the Waldorf, stocking the Myrtle Room with hundreds of nightingales "borrowed" from every zoo in six states. The

Vanderbilts held a little supper and entertained their guests with a mild amusement — an entire Broadway musical.

One of the zanier events of the season may have been the horseback dinner thrown by Cornelius K. G. Billings, to celebrate his new racing stable. Billings hired the topflight restaurant of the time, cleared out all the tables and brought in scores of horses. The guests sat on horseback and dined from high trays brought by waiters dressed as stable grooms. The busboys stood by to remove anything produced by any horse that may have lacked the proper social graces.

And it was not just balls and dinners. Everything was catered. When the Yale-Princeton football game became an "event," three chartered trains with 50 parlor cars headed to New Haven and back. Each car had a distinct menu served going and another coming back with each host trying to outdo the other — and, of course, accompanied by the now compulsory Krug '98.

And all of the above was catered by the one, the only, Louis Sherry. Sherry was an institution at the time. He catered Mrs.

Astor's ball and all the other grand events. It was at his famous restaurant that the horseback dinner was held. It was his waiters who poured the Krug '98 on the football trains. (What? Oh yeah! Yale won 23-4.)

Louis Sherry was not just the preferred caterer of the fabulously wealthy, he was the essential ingredient of the success of any affair. Many of his clients thought it was his special Parisian knack. But Sherry wasn't Parisian; heck, he wasn't even French. Louis Sherry was born in St. Albans, Vermont. But his courtesy, reserve, attention to detail and ability to deliver in even the most chaotic circumstances had clients convinced that it must be a European flair.

Sherry was good at organizing things efficiently yet unobtrusively. So when the great J. P. Morgan needed to be sure that he and a party of 50 might have every need catered to on a private train with 10 personal parlor cars, he would turn to Sherry. And he did rely on Sherry several times. One extraordinary example was the Panic of 1907, when banks and brokerages began to collapse as October began.

Sherry's efficiency and discretion allowed Morgan to work magic in a crisis that had the secretary of the Treasury pleading for someone to save the nation.

The "Panic of 1907" and the roles of J. P. Morgan and Louis Sherry were rather unique in U.S. financial history.

It all happened rather quickly (as noted) in the month of October — strange as that sounds. Up until then, the country and the market had been having a rather remarkable bout of prosperity, and commentators began to talk of a "new era" of good times.

There were several "environmental factors" that made the market ripe for a fall. Money was drawn away by the aftereffects of things like the Sino-Russian War, the Frisco Quake and the usual banking disruptions of the crop cycle (you know — money leaves city banks to go to country banks to pay for harvests).

In mid-October, the catalyst came. Two fellows named Heinze and Morse tried to "corner" a stock called United Copper. They missed!

Now, if you have forgotten your course in Wall Street 101, let's do a refresher on "corners." Not everyone who deals in a stock is a fan who thinks the stock is going up. A few sometimes believe the outlook for a stock is more fable than fact. They think that when folks find out about it, the price

will go down. So they sell stock they don't even own to correct the irrational exuberance that they think they see. Since they don't "own" the stock that they're selling, when it comes time to deliver, they have to borrow it from someone who has it. For that, the "short seller" pays a fee to borrow the stock, hoping to buy it back cheaper later (when it goes down) and pocket the profit.

The problem in that strategy, even if you're right about the company being not so hot, is that, if for some reason there's a sudden rush to buy, the fellow who lent you the stock may demand it back so he can sell it. And if the rush is so great that all the lenders want their stock back, then there is a "corner." That means the short sellers have no way to borrow stock and must pay any price to settle their contract. Thus they are trapped in a corner — with no escape.

But Heinze and Morse failed to buy enough to corner the stock before they themselves ran short of funds. Suddenly the stock turned lower, and they faced "margin calls." Heinze was president of the Mercantile-National Trust Co. Fearing that the bank had been used as a lender to the

"busted corner," depositors began to line up at the door.

The next morning (October 17), the rush was so intense that Heinze resigned as the bank president and put his brokerage firm into bankruptcy. Now the crush turned against Morse. Within 24 hours, he was forced to resign from the banks he controlled. But that was not enough. By the close of business Saturday, there were lines at nearly every bank run by anyone rumored to have been a "Waldorf crony" of Heinze or Morse.

Panic was in the air, and a frantic telegram was sent to the wise and powerful elder statesman of Wall St., J. P. Morgan. The old lion, now in his 70s, was in Virginia at a religious convocation. We don't know what the message was, but surely Morgan the Great could smell panic. He must return immediately. Naturally he turned to — who else — Louis Sherry.

Sherry had accompanied Morgan on the trip. He was there to assure that his men catered the parlor cars properly on the train ride down. He was there to assure that the food and service at the rented estate would be up to Morgan's demands.

And now suddenly he must pack up the

WALL STREET DURING THE PANIC OF 1907.

entire Morgan entourage, including "his Grandness," assorted valets, footmen, etc. and several high bishops who were among the clergy convocating. Then Sherry had to load the whole amalgam back on the private parlor cars on the private train without a hitch. Then all he had to do was to ensure that they were served the first of several elegant meals on the way home. No problem!

The Morgan train arrived on Sunday morning. After a light breakfast, Morgan bid the bishops good day and headed for his mansion on 36th Street. Sherry saw to it that everyone and everything was taken care of.

At his mansion, Morgan discovered that a full-blown bank panic had begun. How and where to stop it was the problem he had to solve. He thanked the assembled bank presidents and officials and sent them off to lunch (probably at Louis Sherry's). Then he sat down to play solitaire. This was how he organized his thoughts — by fixing on the organized progress of the cards. Later all of the cream of high finance returned to his house seeking answers. But there were no answers yet — just coffee, conversation and questions. By midnight, they had left, as had the bringer of late snacks — Louis Sherry.

The next morning, Monday, the panic began anew. Over the weekend, someone had recalled that among the Waldorf Willies who hung out with the bankrupt Morse was Charles Barney. Barney was the president of the Knickerbocker Bank, one of the largest, fastest-growing banks in America. No matter…a crony was still a crony, and soon the Knickerbockers' Board held an emergency "off-site" meeting. Where else but in a private dining room of the restaurant owned by — who else — Louis Sherry.

Unfortunately, a reporter found out about the "secret meeting," and, despite Sherry's best efforts, scores of irate depositors broke into the meeting. So much for saving the Knickerbocker.

The next morning's edition of the New York *Tribune* left little doubt that the Knickerbocker was in trouble. And any doubt that you might harbor disappeared when you read that the new New York State superintendent of banks, a man named Luther Mott, had taken one look at the Knickerbocker's books and resigned immediately.

When the Knickerbocker opened at 10:00 a.m. that morning, hundreds of depositors waited to get their money out. There was a "run" on the bank, and what a run it

was: With the cream of society as its client base, the Knickerbocker found itself with a run that, as one observer said, looked more like an opera opening. Ladies and gentlemen in the finest of finery came to collect, or at least protect, their life savings.

As the doors opened, they cheerily marched in. They remained friendly, even supportive, but they were insistent on getting money. In a scene that a later generation would associate with George Bailey in *It's a Wonderful Life*, management attempted to reassure, calm or even persuade depositors to take only a portion of their funds. However, even in the "Ladies Department" the call to "relax" was not selling. (Yes, there was a separate section of the bank for ladies so that they need not brush up against "men" while transacting their business. This was true at nearly all banks at the time.)

By late morning, it became evident that the great Knickerbocker Bank would not have the success of the later, cinematic Bailey Building and Loan. In late morning, a senior official climbed on a chair and announced "No further payments today." The frocked and jeweled but now penniless depositors were led out the doors, and a great national bank panic ensued. Thanks to the telegraph the panic stretched from

coast to coast by the next day.

Charles Barney would commit suicide, but that only worsened the panic.

Like most bank panics, this one had aspects that would have been zany were it not for the fact that people were hurt by their consequences. For example, there was a run on a bank in the north end of Manhattan. The line got so long it stretched all the way down the block until some of the folks seemed to be lined up in front of a different bank on the far corner. Soon there was a run on that bank. When a newspaper ran a picture of a run on a Harlem savings bank, depositors read it as The Harlem Savings Bank and rushed to get their money out of that institution.

Instantly, the banks were in panic, Wall Street was in panic, New York City was in panic, and the country was in panic. The secretary of the Treasury (United States Division) knew there was only one man to stem the tide. It clearly was J. P. Morgan. He sent a telegram telling Morgan he would be on the next train. Morgan called the key bankers to meet at his mansion, but first he called in Louis Sherry to cater and care for his meetings — first with the Treasury head and then with the bankers.

Over the next week, and more Morgan masterfully fought off each new thrust of panic. The saving banks, the trust companies, even the stock market. Each time, there were key meetings of key people, sometimes all evening long and often into the early morning. Through it all, J. P. Morgan was magnificent (but so too was Louis Sherry, who quietly, unobtrusively made sure the surroundings allowed the titans to stay on task.)

So Morgan might listen, quiz, listen and then retire to his "mind-organizing solitaire" knowing that the captains of finance were being cared for (and kept captive) by the services of a staff supervised by Sherry. Despite the deftness, determination and discretion of this duo their battle stayed defensive until the stock market nearly spun out of control.

The wariness of the threatened banks made money available to brokers very scarce. So, down on the floor of the Stock Exchange, at a place called the "money desk" (under the main arch between the "Main Room" and the "garage") the rate for "call money" was very tight. Call money was a kind of margin loan available to brokerage firms. The money desk was a long mahogany desk where wealthy elder bro-

kers (tired of racing about) might lend margin to brokers trying to finance their positions. In a mark of high technology, the call rate (price of money) was flashed on an electronic board that hung above the arch (careful observers will note the screws and fittings are still there). On the fifth day of the panic the marvelous sign read 100 — meaning 100 percent margin — meaning if you wanted to borrow a dollar, you had to put up a dollar as collateral. Therefore, you could not borrow unless you could prove you didn't need to borrow.

The market went into a nosedive. In fact, the NYSE president went across the street to tell Morgan that the Exchange would have to close. Knowing a trading halt would compound the panic, Morgan acted quickly, pledging $20 million to ensure the market remained open. It worked. Prices began to firm. As one newspaper would note that night, "Morgan Saves Market."

But that evening, the meeting at Morgan's mansion in the East 30s was rather somber. The bank runs continued, and now the market might fail. Sherry's staff quietly moved among the bank presidents and other titans of finance, all of whom awaited a master stroke from the genius, Morgan. Among the somber faces was a new one, a lawyer named Cass

Ledyard. Ledyard brought even more bad news. His client, the prestigious brokerage firm of Moore & Schley was about to go under. Their only collateral was a majority share in the Tennessee Coal and Iron Company. It was a fine company but had no liquid market for its shares. We can only imagine the groans.

Morgan retired for some mind-clearing solitaire while Sherry catered to the guests. Suddenly, amid the methodical placement of the cards, it dawned on Morgan; Tennessee Coal and Iron had the kind of reserves that could make Morgan's newly formed U.S. Steel Company the greatest steel maker in the world.

In a matter of minutes, he explained his brainstorm to his aides. In a matter of hours, they turned it into an effective but complex proposal to save the market and the banks. In a matter of days, Morgan convinced the government not to attack the proposal on antitrust grounds, lest the panic resume.

The market rallied. The lines in front of the banks disappeared. And Morgan became even wealthier, as U.S. Steel surged. But he certainly seemed to deserve it. He knew the right caterer to pick in a panic.

LIGHTING UP THE MOVEMENT

As we've noted in some previous tales, food and finance have shared a long and interesting history, particularly around Wall Street. But, as in any lasting relationship, there have been bumps along the way, and some problems have a familiar ring to them.

You've probably noticed, either personally or through the headlines, the topic of smoking in public tends to ignite heated debate. All across New York, restaurants, bars and even a few luncheon clubs are wrestling with ways to best serve all their clients — smoker and nonsmoker alike.

But this is not the first time that New Yorkers dining out have grappled with smoking and the law. There was the famous "Sullivan Law" (no, not the one banning concealed weapons cited in so many gangster movies). This particular statute was passed by New York City Alderman Sullivan in January 1908.

Sullivan and supporters feared that public smoking not only scandalized observers but contributed to the delinquency of the smoker. So, the New York City government banned public smoking — by women!

The very day after passage, a policeman spotted a young lady, named Katie Mulcahey, coming out of a Bowery Bistro. She struck a match against the wall and began to light a cigarette. The officer rushed up and explained that the new law forbade ladies to smoke in public places. According to press reports of the time, Miss Mulcahey said several things to the policeman. Among the more printable was: "No man shall dictate to me!" (Has a familiar ring to it, I think!)

Miss Mulcahey then began puffing away, prompting the unnamed officer to haul her into night court before Judge Kernochan. Having determined that she was "Miss" Mulcahey, the judge fined her $5.00 (a week's salary at the time). When she was unable to pay, he ordered her to a holding cell. Perversely, among the few possessions she was allowed to take with her were the cigarettes and matches.

The next morning, the board of aldermen awoke to mocking headlines and threats of demonstrations. In a hurriedly called meeting, the aldermen fearlessly declared the law valid but determined that it was up to restaurant, hotel and club managers to enforce it (some things never change).

Interestingly, the vote was not unanimous. Alderman O'Doul warned his fellows that the furor over this law could lead women to band together and push for equality — perhaps the vote — and more. History doesn't tell us if O'Doul used his foresight in the stock market.

Anyway, Miss Mulcahey was released, the women's movement energized, New York City changed its form of government and the convivial culinary crowd got back to just worrying about victuals and vintages — for the time at least.

AN ADVERTISEMENT FOR PREFERRED STOCK CIGARETTES.

In 1914, the simmering jealousy and suspicion that had long marked European politics boiled over with the assassination of Emperor Franz Joseph in Sarajevo. Soon alliances were formed, demands leveled and troops dispatched. At first everyone thought it was all "posturing" — that someone would back down. Nations were clearly too enlightened to march into a global conflict that could ruin them all. Weren't they??

But by July, it became obvious that no one had sense enough to stop. As war became more certain, one of the first casualties was finance. Panic selling began to hit stock exchanges around the world. One after another, they were shuttered.

Montreal, Madrid, Brussels, Budapest, Berlin, Rome, Russia were closed, then finally London. Now the New York Stock Exchange stood alone, the last liquid market still open. The world now had only one outlet to sell stocks. No one market could bail out the world, however.

On the morning of July 31, the NYSE governors met and voted not to open. The NYSE would stay closed for four and one-half months. When it reopened, it did so with collars or restraints on price movements.

The U.S. (and Wall Street) watched the early stages of the tragic war with somewhat of a neutral eye. (There was a huge German population, after all.) Wall Street had a bit more of a British leaning due to the London connection and the massive English investments in the U.S. So great was the involvement that the NYSE shut down *twice* on the death of King Edward VII in 1910. Once at 11a.m. on May 7 at the news of his death, and again on May 20th from 10 to 12 for his funeral. Eight years earlier, on August 9, 1902, the Exchange had closed on a Saturday for his coronation.

As the war wore on, however, the desperate moves of the German military (especially the sinking of the *Lusitania* in 1915) began to shift even public opinion in favor of Britain and her allies. The populace, including German-Americans, shifted from things German — sauerkraut was being renamed "victory cabbage."

In 1917, the U.S. entered the war. Hundreds of NYSE members and clerks resigned to serve in the army (some did not live to see victory).

Others served elsewhere. One member, Bernard Baruch, resigned to run several government war efforts. Older members, rebuffed for active service, joined the Red Cross to help the effort. There were over 100 such volunteers.

Finally, on November 7, 1918, word swept the floor that an armistice was signed, ending the war. Cheers went up on the Exchange. Prices started to soar. The Exchange closed to celebrate the peace.

But no announcement of peace came forth. Papers headlined: "Wall Street Buys False Armistice." Later, observers would suggest that an armistice had, in fact, been agreed to on November 7. But government officials (of some government or several) had bowed to the symmetry, or numerology, or some lucky charm and delayed the announcement until the 11th hour of the 11th day of the 11th month (November 11, 1918).

Whatever the reason, peace finally came and Wall Street found itself, suddenly, the new money center of the world.

No history of New York City and finance would be complete without taking note of a remarkable man named "Ivy Lee," who was, perhaps, the first of the modern "spin doctors."

Lee thought of himself as a public relations man, but he was far more. Anybody can get you publicity, but to change a negative image around to a positive one takes a special kind of genius.

The poor, misunderstood billionaire who hired Ivy to help him out was a gent named John D. Rockefeller. He personally felt he had acquired his billions through hard work and native peasant cunning.

The newspapers of the time, however, mistook his success to be the result of extortion, deception, connivance, fraud and, occasionally, outright theft. In addition, they felt he had done some bad things on the side.

Rockefeller had begun his climb in that place where so many great American legends have *begun* or *ended* — Cleveland, Ohio. (Yes, this is a history of New York, but you do need background.)

A few years earlier, Rockefeller (an earnest bookkeeper in his 20s) had been asked by his employers to evaluate the

ON APRIL 2, 1903, THE NYSE MOVED INTO ITS NEW HOME AT 18 BROAD STREET.

investment opportunities of something called "oil." Rockefeller dutifully trekked to the oil fields in western Pennsylvania newly discovered by Edwin Drake. Rockefeller, just as dutifully reported back to his employers that no one would ever make

money in oil. The investors moved off. Prices in the oil fields collapsed. And yet someone began buying these bankruptcy bargains. That man's name was Rockefeller.

Before he was 30 years old, he somehow managed to acquire nearly half the oil-refining capacity in the U.S. He was almost indicted when his outfit, The Southern Improvement Company, was charged with blackmailing railroads into illegal kickbacks not only on his shipments but also on his competitor's shipments. (P. S. — the details on these latter kickbacks told him what his competitors were shipping, to whom and at what price.) Rockefeller must have figured the prosecutors didn't like the company name, so he reincorporated as Standard Oil of Cleveland.

Now things got interesting. By his 40th birthday, Rockefeller controlled 95 percent of all the refinery capacity in the country. Outrage erupted. Critics claimed Rockefeller was buying whole legislatures and sabotaging competitors, while extorting kickbacks from buyers and customers alike. Rockefeller responded by reinventing the company as a "trust."

Over the next several decades, enormous wealth poured in, but so did enormous hatred. In fact, for many years, public polls showed Standard Oil to be the most hated company in America.

Then came the "Ludlow Strike."

A group of miners at one of Rockefeller's interests began a strike. As the strike dragged on, they were forced to move their families to a tent city in a field nearby.

Newspapers of the day said that Rockefeller sent hired thugs in to destroy the tent city. Whoever sent whom — the result was a national uproar calling for Rockefeller's scalp (literally) and the breakup of his empire.

Enter: Ivy Lee.

His client is the most hated man in America running the most hated company in America. Press conferences won't help. Endorsements won't help. Apologies (even if you could get them) won't help. You'll have to resort to that superweapon of public relations — the gimmick.

Lee figured there wasn't a dime's worth of difference between his heavily hated client and your average crotchety grandpa. To prove it, he made sure that whenever Rockefeller saw a child under 12 years, old John D. would stop and grandly give the child a shiny dime. Ivy Lee even waived the age limit for newsboys and shoeshine boys. Then he would tip photographers that Rockefeller might be in the neighborhood that day.

So the photographers began following the old geezer around, hoping to catch him buying a legislature or extorting a railroad. But Rockefeller just went from meeting to meeting — pausing only to give newsboys and small children shiny new dimes. Well, if

you've been toting a heavy camera all day, you've gotta shoot something. Soon there were almost daily shots of an elderly Rockefeller handing dimes to tiny tots and newsboys.

Originally, the papers ran the photos as a knock. You know, "Robber Baron Billionaire Gives Dime to Kid." But Ivy Lee told him not to stop, and after many months of such photos, the public began to wonder if the old guy had a kind streak. Suddenly, he was acceptable, even benevolent. (A few charities he started didn't hurt either.) Thus, Ivy Lee gave the most hated man in America a new credibility.

JOHN D. ROCKEFELLER SR.
GIVING A DIME TO HIS CADDY.

On September 16, 1920, sometime before noon, a drayhorse hitched to an enclosed wagon stood, unattended, pawing the ground (or cobblestones) at the curbside in front of the U.S. Assay Office on Wall Street.

It was a cloudy, somewhat humid day, and brokers and clerks at the New York Stock Exchange began setting up lunch reliefs amid a mild rally in moderate trading. The rally's key feature was Reading Railroad, up about 2, at 93 3/4. The other feature was U.S. Steel (trading steadily at 89 3/8). Many clerks tended to spend the lunch hour watching the excavation for the NYSE annex, at Broad and Wall, right next to the Exchange itself. (It would soon house "the Garage").

Just minutes before noon, and just minutes before Exchange clerks and other clerks from the House of Morgan (just across Broad Street from the Exchange) might have poured out to the corner of Broad and Wall, a huge explosion erupted from the wagon. It killed 30 people on the street instantly, and injured hundreds of others.

Flying metal shards tore into the lime-stone face of the Morgan Bank, dislodged steps on the Subtreasury next to the Assay Office and even shot through the window of the Bankers Club at 120 Broadway (one block away and 30 stories above the explosion).

Luckily, the drapes on the grand windows of the Exchange were closed, so none of the flying glass killed anyone in the "Reading" crowd.

Nevertheless, Bill Remick, the Exchange president, walked to the rostrum from the money desk and range the bell, halting trading for the day. He said he did it because it was "just the right thing to do." (Where are they now?)

No one ever caught the bomber, despite the final death toll of scores of people. And the next morning, the rally resumed, beginning the upswing of the Roaring Twenties. Years later, but before the crash, an attorney general would remark that the bomb had been planted by those who believed in communism.

To understand how powerful the bomb was, stroll over and look at the pock marks that still sit in the wall of the Morgan Guaranty on the corner of Wall and Broad.

THE EXPLOSION KILLED 30 ON THE STREET BUT THE NYSE'S HEAVY BROCADE CURTAINS KEPT FLYING GLASS FROM INJURING THOSE INSIDE.

Hollywood has given us hundreds of images of the "Roaring Twenties." In fact, they titled at least one movie just that. We've seen the image — no rules, bobbed hair, short skirts, bathtub gin and, of course, Tommy guns. Then, naturally, the crash and retribution.

But if there ever was a symbol of the 1920s, it wasn't James Cagney nor George Raft. It was a transplanted Bostonian who refused to be boxed-in by Middle America opportunities. This fellow didn't just symbolize the Roaring Twenties, he may have caused it — at least where Wall Street is concerned. His name was William Crapo Durant.

Billy Durant spent the first 25 years of his life in dead-end jobs — grocer's clerk, insurance salesman, medicine peddler, etc. But his dreams were larger by far. Somehow, he begged, borrowed and cajoled his friends into a stake in a wagon company. His organizational talents showed, and soon he had several factories. Success was his.

But in 1903, someone introduced Durant to a fellow named Dave Buick. Dave had an idea, as did a few others, to put a small gasoline engine in a horse wagon and skip the horse. Billy Durant knew an Internet idea when he saw one. He started building Buicks using his carriage mass-production expertise. Soon Durant was buying up the operations of guys named Olds, Cadillac and Oakland. Hoping to keep the model names, he called the combination General Motors.

Durant's genius and aggressiveness succeeded so well that by 1909, he was offered the opportunity to buy the Ford Motor Company for under $10 million. (Ford had over-borrowed to compete with Durant.)

Unfortunately, GM's bankers refused to lend Durant the money for the Ford takeover. Worse yet, they figured that if the great Ford was pinched, Durant must have overestimated the car business. Therefore, they opted to call all his loans, which left him penniless and put the bankers in charge of GM.

(Hang on — we're almost to the "Twenties".)

Durant, began to beg and borrow from friends again. This time it was to buy the concept of a low-cost car to compete with Ford. The idea belonged to a guy named Louis Chevrolet. This was around 1912 (just two years since the banks had bumped Durant at GM).

Soon the new "Chevrolet" was bringing Durant millions, and he began buying GM shares on the NYSE. After he had a core position, he bid for control of GM. He offered four Chevrolet shares for every GM share. He strode into the GM boardroom to regain control. Hold it!…The vote is a tie. Both sides have an equal amount.

That's when John Raskob and the DuPont family stepped forward and voted with Durant (who happened to be the guy who had advised them to buy GM years before — when he, Durant, was chairman).

With the popular Chevrolet now in the fold and Durant's optimistic genius back at the helm, GM began to really grow.

Durant added one more unlikely product, however. Some friends asked for a loan to support an experimental idea. It was an "electric ice box" being developed by the Guardian Frigerator Company. Durant saw Internet II and bought the company product, which he named a "Frigidiare."

Things were going great, and Durant sought more money to kick things into high gear. But it was the year 1920. Post-World War I enthusiasm had finally made money tight.

WILLIAM DURANT WITH A DURANT MOTORS STAR.

"To hell with the bankers," thought Durant. "I'll go to the marketplace itself." Durant was, and would prove himself to be, a great trader. But he appears to have been a rather lousy investment banker.

GM needed about $70 million. The stock was selling around $38. Durant raised half the money by selling quietly to a British syndicate at $20 a share. It may not have been as quiet as Durant thought. GM stock began to drop through $30. He sought to sell the balance of the underwriting to a U.S. syndicate (again at $20). But these underwriters asked for a bonus — options on a block at $10. Again word leaked out. GM shares plunged.

Durant had pledged his own shares as collateral on loans for money which he used to try to support GM stock. He failed and it failed. He went from being worth $100 million (several billion today) to owing $30 million (not nice whatever the decade). Even his pal Raskob knew that Durant had to step down for the good of GM. He was given an option on GM but the market would have to soar to give it any value.

So here was William Crapo Durant, the optimistic genius who had made and lost

(more than once) several billion dollars in today's terms, suddenly dead broke again. (He did have a few friends with dough — Raskob, the DuPonts and lots of early backers). He also found some help from a few former coworkers. Actually, they were a bit more than coworkers. They had been co-billionaires. They were the Fisher brothers.

The Fisher brothers had built horse carriages as Durant had in the beginning. But the Fisher brothers carriages were so elegant that "Body by Fisher" became a trademark. And when General Motors bought out their biggest "body" supplier, they paid a record amount, leaving the Fisher brothers with time on their hands and many billions in today's dollars to fret about. The next line was obvious: "Let's go see old Billy Durant who we hear went someplace called 'Wall Street.'"

Durant became the mastermind of several bull "pools." The pools were syndicates of traders who usually pooled their money (or their positions) in one or two stocks at a time. Durant's syndicates were extraordinary since they had the Fisher money, the Raskob money and lots of others from the GM gang. Their capital was huge.

They could, and often did, move the price of a target stock 50 or 100 points in a day.

Durant's pools were so popular (and successful) that many of the legendary Wall Street traders of the day joined in. Jesse Livemore, the great trader, or Arthur Cutten, the wizard of the grain pits, might join. Even Al Smith, the potential candidate for president, joined in. Soon, mere rumors that Durant was in a stock was enough to shoot prices higher. Durant was credited or blamed for causing much of the frenzy that was the wild bull market of 1920s.

Durant became concerned in early 1929 about the Fed and what it might cause the market to do. He even went to the White House in April to warn President Hoover. But Durant figured he and his cronies were too smart to be crushed when the crash came. He was wrong. And again he was penniless.

Durant never recouped his fortune or his fame. But just before he died, he was promoting an idea for the growth of leisure time after World War II. He suggested there would be great growth in, of all things, bowling alleys. Backers thought he was crazy…and ignored him.

THE THREE BEARS CATCH GOLDILOCKS

On Thursday, October 24, 1929, Wall Street brokers headed for work more than a little confused. The action the day before had made them a bit uneasy. Several weeks earlier, on September 3, the day after Labor Day, in fact, the Dow had made one more record high — the latest of a series in a super bull market that had lasted years and caught the attention of a fascinated public. Then the market began to sputter — but so what. The Great Bull had rolled and rested before, only to roar and rise again. But the prior day's trading had raised the anxiety level.

So on this Thursday morning, the market opened nervous but relatively steady. Within the first half hour, prices began to fade, and the tape began to run late. By noon, the tape was nearly an hour and a half late in reporting transactions in a market that had opened only two hours before. To speed the reporting, digits were deleted and so "Radio," which had opened at 68 3/4 now showed on the tape at "8 3/4." But prices were moving so fast that the price was not 58 3/4 but 48 3/4 on its way

to 48 1/4 before it would bottom in the afternoon at 44 1/2. To avoid confusion, the Exchange published flash prices of selected securities on the slower-moving bond tape.

By early afternoon, the cascade of prices caused an emergency meeting at the offices of J. P. Morgan across the street from the Exchange. The heads of all the big banks were there: Mitchell of Citibank; Presser of Bankers Trust; Wiggin of Chase; Potter of the Guaranty Trust; Baker of First National; and, of course, Lamont of the House of Morgan. They pledged over $30 million and called the "Morgan broker," Richard Whitney, who got the job by cleverly being the brother of one of the senior partners at Morgan.

Some broker looked out the windows on Broad Street and noticed the major bankers of America were going into the

House of Morgan. Not understanding the penalty for inside information, he probably said "The bankers are meeting to form a pool." Despite the fact that no one would use such tainted data, prices began to steady.

And then Whitney entered the U.S. Steel crowd and bid 205 for 10,000. He bought only a few hundred shares but left his bid on the book. He then walked to each of the high-profile stocks of that era and bid similarly. The market began to rally. In the final half-hour, selling began again, but a disaster had been averted. At the bell, the tape was four hours late and the volume was an astounding 12 million shares. Papers headlined — "Bankers Save the Day."

Four days later, the bottom would fall out of the market. Four months later, banks would begin to fail. And 10 years later, Richard Whitney, whose celebrity had made him the president of the Exchange, would be sent to Sing Sing prison for misappropriating money escrowed for widows of Exchange members. The 1930s were not the Roaring Twenties.

STOCK PRICES OBVIOUSLY FELL BEFORE ART PRICES.

RICHARD WHITNEY, CIRCA 1932.

Richard Whitney's fall from grace is one of the most stunning in financial history. As the visible operative of the bankers pool during the crash, he was seen as a hero who almost turned the tide single-handedly. The story of his dramatic bid of "205 for 10,000 Steel" reached nearly mythic proportions.

As "the man who almost stopped the crash," he was revered in some financial circles as though he were a valiant general whose courage and leadership nearly gained the day against overwhelming forces. People began to talk as though Whitney had used his own money in an attempt to save America.

This notoriety helped get him elected president of the NYSE from 1930 to 1935. Even after he left that office, he was seen as the "Spokesman of Wall Street" (meant in the best of ways). In fact, Whitney was a much sought-after speaker on topics like "Business Honesty." He was also the point man against "radical" suggestions from the newly formed SEC.

But Whitney's financial underpinnings were beginning to unravel. A few escapades in Florida real estate and a bad "post-Prohibition" investment turned very sour. He was in a cash bind. First he borrowed from friends. Then he borrowed from the upwardly mobile (young brokers so honored to be seen with Whitney's hand on their shoulder, they were very happy to advance him a bit).

But these stopgap loans could not fill the widening chasm in his cash flow.

Whitney began to dip into funds he was supposed to protect. Among these were the New York Yacht Club and the NYSE Gratuity Fund. (Dedicated to the widows and orphans of members.)

Ironically, it was an NYSE review that tripped him up. His misuse of funds was exposed. Despite attempts for more time from old friends, on March 8, 1938, President Gay mounted the Exchange rostrum and rang the bell once. Then, he announced to the astonished and silent membership that Richard Whitney and company was suspended for "conduct inconsistent with just and equitable principles of trade." To add to the irony, the leader of the WASP old guard was expelled as a member on St. Patrick's Day.

One last note on Whitney. From the day he entered Sing Sing prison until his parole in summer of 1941, everyone — from the lowest prisoner, to the guards and even the warden — addressed him as "Mr. Whitney." The image of a fallen hero is not totally erased.

The man who would replace, and in some ways surpass, Richard Whitney as the leader of Wall Street was about as opposite as could be imagined.

John A. Coleman was the son of a New York City policeman. He was certainly no Ivy Leaguer. He began his career at the NYSE at the lowest level. No one would ever see him as an urbane sophisticate. In fact, he might accuse someone who "put on airs" as a phony, trying to be a real "Charlie Potatoes."

Coleman was very many things that Whitney was not. Coleman was Irish, he was Catholic and he was a Democrat. He was extremely active in each of these institutions.

As an Irishman, a Democrat and a Catholic, he naturally became a close friend of Governor Alfred E. Smith, who ran for President in 1928. Smith and Coleman were also close friends of John Raskob, who, you may recall, made millions in the 1920s.

John Coleman's career at the NYSE bordered on the meteoric at a time when apprenticeship was the rule of the day. He began as a page or squad boy in 1916. Within eight years, he was a member of the Exchange. A few years later, he had his own firm. And in the year of transition, 1938, he became a governor of the Exchange just at the time that scandal would ruin Whitney.

Whitney and Coleman were very different in one other way. Whitney did not avoid the press: in fact, he seemed to bask in the fame and notoriety he found. Like some of today's titans, he found good press clippings sometimes lead to good credit ratings. (And Whitney needed credit credibility.)

Coleman, however, shunned the public limelight. He believed that fame was not necessary for influence and power. And, in his case, he was right. Coleman's influence might seem incredible to those who did not know him.

When he was married in 1930, he was worried that he might not get from St. Aloysius's Church in Jersey City to the elegant reception at the Park Lane in New York on time. So he called his Democratic friends, Alfred E. Smith and Frank Hague, mayor of Jersey City and one of the most powerful political bosses in America. Not only did each of these powerhouses arrange for multiple motorcycle escorts in their respective states; they arranged to shut down the Holland Tunnel so the wedding entourage might pass through unencumbered.

Working in Democratic circles and Irish societies, Coleman came to know virtually every labor leader and political leader on a first-name basis. For decades, he was called as an informal mediator to head off a strike or settle a dispute.

Wall Street legend says that one mayor of New York was advised by Cardinal Spellman that his best and perhaps only hope of avoiding a subway strike was to have John Coleman intervene. (The mayor almost blew it by forgetting to send a car to bring Coleman to City Hall.)

John Coleman was chairman of the NYSE from 1943 to 1946, but for four decades, virtually nothing could be done on Wall Street without his approval.

He spoke with a nasal Lower East Side accent that often caused people to mistake his quick, clever, Irish wit for a mere wise-crack.

Coleman's influence in Democratic circles and Wall Street was mammoth. His influence in the Catholic Church was almost astounding. Raising millions for its hospitals and schools, he was at every event related to the Church — usually on the dais.

In 1965, when Pope Paul VI visited New York, Wall Streeters smiled knowingly as on their flickering TV screens, they saw the pontiff greeted at the steps of the plane by John Coleman. The next day, as the pope's mass from Yankee Stadium was televised, the most prominent figure beside the pontiff was John Coleman, as chief altar-server decked out in the medieval garb of a Knight of Saint Gregory. Finally, as the pope left New York City, he was escorted to the plane's steps by John Coleman. The pope ascended the steps, turned, then came back down to confer with Coleman. Wall Street thought the pontiff may have had one last question.

Chroniclers of Wall Street have sometimes noted that the 1920s saw the emergence of the Irish in the world of finance. Names like Joe Kennedy, Mike Meehan, "Sell 'em Ben" Smith and scores of others. But none was less publicly known — nor more influential — than John Aloysius Coleman.

DEPICTION OF WHAT
THINGS WERE LIKE WHEN
COLEMAN STARTED.

CHRISTMAS IS STILL CHRISTMAS

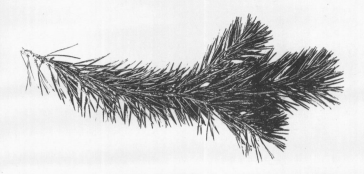

On December 23, 1931, America was spiraling into the depths of the Depression. Thousands of banks had closed, and there was a national panic that more closings might be imminent. And large corporations announced huge layoff programs, stunning many who thought they were safe. Those who had a job were grateful just to be employed.

Among those were a group of construction workers in NYC. As they stood amidst the rubble of demolished buildings in midtown Manhattan, they talked of how lucky they were that some rich guy had hired them for a new but risky development. And since it was near Christmas, they decided to celebrate the fact that they had a job.

They got an 18-foot Christmas tree from a guy in a lot on the corner who apparently had discovered that folks with apartments suitable for 18-foot trees were not too free with the green pictures of dead presidents in 1931. So the workers stood the big tree up in the rubble and decorated it with tin cans and other items in the lot. A photographer saw it as a perfect symbol of 1931. It caught on immediately, and each Christmas as the project proceeded a new tree was put up. And even after the project (Rockefeller Center) was completed, management put up a new (and much bigger) tree each year. The tradition continues to today — but perhaps you knew that.

A DAY TO LIVE IN INFAMY

The winds of war had been blowing in Europe from the mid-1930s on. And, in their own way, they blew some prosperity back to America and to Wall Street. The need for goods and even armaments in Europe restarted American factories and stimulated the general economy. Things were going right but for the wrong reasons.

Still not healed from the Great War two decades before, America's war-weary memory dragged on the hopes and joys of workers called back to work. The lessons of attempted non-involvement haunted this stirring workforce.

The chill of concern turned to a freeze on December 7, 1941, as Japanese planes strafed and bombed the cream of the U.S. Pacific fleet. The attack had come on a Sunday. Immediately, there were press and private calls to shut down the Exchange — as it had done in 1914. The NYSE, like much of America, had suspected that war might be coming. It had discussed what course was best for America and for investors. It had determined to try to stay open.

So on Monday, December 8, 1941, the NYSE opened at 10:00 a.m. on schedule. Prices did fall. The Dow dropped over 3

IN JULY 1943, THE FIRST
FEMALE EMPLOYEES OF
THE NYSE POSE AT A
TRADING POST.

percent — but in light volume and without panic. The market would remain open throughout the war.

Its president, William McChesney Martin, was drafted in 1941. He resigned from the NYSE and, like hundreds of members, clerks and employees, went off to serve his country. The Exchange knew it had lost a great leader. (Martin would go on to be one of the most effective Federal Reserve chairmen in history.)

To avoid having its next president drafted away, they chose the post-middle-age Emil Schram — a Roosevelt appointee who had headed the Reconstruction Finance Agency.

The war did not bring either interest or activity to the Exchange. Every spare dime that America and Wall street had was rushed into war bonds. The NYSE hosted many rallies.

The war bond effort ground Wall Street activity to a virtual standstill. Seat prices fell rapidly. In 1942, they fell to $17,000 per seat.

This raised some eyebrows since the Gratuity Fund (death benefit to widows or children of members) was $20,000. Some members noted that the disparity meant you were worth more dead than alive. Enlistments continued to grow — hopefully not in response to the arbitrage.

Even with the low, low activity, the manpower shift left some gaps. So, flying in the face of nearly 150 years of tradition, women were introduced to the floor. They were usually found in noninteractive roles (at $20 or $25 per week) so that the harshness of trading (and traders) would not stress them.

When the war ended, America felt that its returning veterans should find waiting the jobs they had left to defend America. Everywhere, women were thanked and dismissed. "Rosie the Riveter" and Rosie the Exchange reporter were both sent home. Main Street and Wall Street returned to being male domains.

ONE OF THE GAPING HOLES LEFT BY THE B-25 BOMBER.

On July 28, 1945, a heavy fog hung over the not-so-busy streets of Manhattan on a Saturday morning. The observation deck of the Empire State Building was deserted, which was a lucky turn of events since it held down the casualties when a B-25 army bomber lost in the fog plowed into the 79th floor of the building (and stuck there).

The bomber had been scheduled to land at LaGuardia, but due to the dense fog, it was diverted toward Newark. The pilot apparently didn't realize that the New York skyline lay in between the two points (or had never seen a silo above three stories). He was actually climbing when he plowed into the Catholic War Relief Offices on the 79th floor.

One of the plane's engines actually plowed right through the building and came out the other side. The plane's fuselage hung eerily and precariously from the side of the skyscraper, looking like some third-rate special effects movie. The crew of three was killed in the crash and resultant fire. Eleven others died, mostly young women in the Catholic War Relief Office.

There was a miracle survivor, however. Her name was Mary Scannell. She was the elevator operator in car number seven. When the plane struck the building, she and her elevator car were on the 80th floor. The jolt snapped the elevator loose and it plunged all the way to the basement. Somehow she survived. Celebrity in 1945 was not quite the way it is now. Scannell's moment of fame came nearly a year later — she appeared on *I've got a Secret*.

To note the anniversary, remember the motto "turn left at the Chrysler Building." (And we hope you'll see King Kong in a new light.)

THE MOST DREADFUL WEEK I CAN RECALL

The last half of November in 1963 did not hold much promise for Wall Street. On Monday the 18th, rumors began to circulate that one or more brokerage firms were in some difficulty. It soon became clear who one of them was. Ira Haupt and Co. withdrew from a blue-ribbon syndicate scheduled to underwrite a large municipal bond issue.

By Tuesday afternoon it became evident that Ira Haupt was on the verge of collapse due to one very large customer. The customer was the Allied Crude Vegetable Oil Refining Company, run by a man named Tino De Angelis. Allied had over $19 million in margin at Haupt and would default as it declared bankruptcy.

The Haupt partners had believed that the margin was collateralized by tanks and tanks of oil stored in tank farms in Bayonne, New Jersey. They even verified the presence of the oil by sending earnest young executives to Bayonne to climb up on the tanks and insert 15-foot "dip sticks" in the center hole. Always, they read "Full."

But the tanks were actually all empty, and there was no collateral for the $19 million debt.

Later testimony would claim that Mr. De Angelis may have put a kind of PCV-style pipe in the center hole and then filled that with oil: thus, the "Full" readings by the bright young executives. (None of these classroom wizards had kicked the tanks, which might have produced a hollow sound.)

The default of Allied was a total surprise to Haupt. Just a week before, it had promoted several people to "partner" based on the assumed prosperity.

Wall Street scrambled to find a solution to keep the Haupt firm viable, as well as another broker for Allied, J. R. Williston and Beane. (Ironically, Beane had been Merrill Lynch Pierce, Fenner and *Beane* until he set out for new adventures and a new partner.)

Friday morning, there was still some hope of salvage. But, by Friday afternoon, hopes were shot, and so was Haupt. They were shot by Lee Harvey Oswald, in a place far from Wall Street.

The tale was told in a chilling series of headlines that rang out on the Dow Jones news tickers in offices all across Wall Street that Friday afternoon.

In those days you had to walk over to the news ticker to read it. To get your attention the ticker would ring a bell on "hot" or "headline" news.

Shortly after 1:30 p.m., the headline bell range three quick times (very big news). "Dateline: Dallas. Shot reported fired at President's Motorcade." Stocks began to sell off. These were missile crisis days. Was there a conspiracy?

An agonizing pause. Three more quick bells. "President Kennedy reported hit." Prices fall further.

A few moments later the headline bell clangs again. "President taken to Parkland Hospital." Anxiety rose, but prices did not.

Finally, another series of bells. "President Kennedy reported dead!" That was about 2:00 p.m.

At 2:07 p.m., the Exchange gong sounded a single loud note (a signal to halt trading and usually an ominous sign). Traders and clerks immediately ceased their dealings and turned to face the rostrum. Senior officials announced that the board of governors had voted to close. It was only the second time in its history that the Exchange had aborted a session for bad news. The first had been the bomb blast in 1920.

The mood was solemn. Conversation was subdued. Affairs were put in order, and people quietly filed out of the building — not knowing what the weekend would bring. A few people were certain of the outcome. They were those recent, hopeful partners of Haupt. Their fate was sealed. As one of them may have remarked, "this is the most dreadful week I can recall."

The nation would survive, as would Wall Street. And Wall Street, as it always does, searched for things to learn. In doing so, it was among the first to stumble on a particularly odd series of coincidences between the shootings of two American presidents. These became known as the Lincoln/Kennedy oddities.

Jack Kennedy's personal secretary was named Lincoln...just as Abe Lincoln's secretary was named Kennedy. Both secretaries had pleaded with their bosses not to go to the place where they were shot. Both presidents were succeeded by guys named Johnson. Both Johnsons were Southerners and former senators. Both Johnsons were born 100 years apart. Kennedy and Lincoln were elected 100 years apart. John Wilkes Booth and Lee Harvey Oswald were born 100 years apart. Both Kennedy and Lincoln were assassinated on a Friday while sitting

TRADING WAS HALTED ON NOVEMBER 22, 1963, WHEN IT WAS CONFIRMED THAT PRESIDENT JOHN F. KENNEDY HAD BEEN ASSASSINATED.

next to their wives. Booth shot Lincoln in a theater and tried to hide in a warehouse. Oswald was in a warehouse when he shot Kennedy, and he then tried to hide in a theater.

But the greatest oddity or irony of all had nothing to do with Lincoln. It had been raining in Dallas on the morning of

November 22nd. Mrs. Kennedy and Texas Governor Connelly's wife had suggested putting the "bubble top" on the limo. At the last minute, the president ordered it removed, so he could wave to the crowd. With the bubble top on, Oswald almost certainly would have missed his chance or his target.

IT TAKES A GOOD SALSA TO MAKE A REAL PARTY!

In the 1970s, the colors of clothes and vans may have been psychedelic, but on Wall Street the mood was blue. That's because at many corporations the bottom line was red.

Inflation had spun out of control. The Japanese were out-producing, outselling and out-saving us everywhere. Social Security recipients marched on Washington to have their benefits "indexed" to prevent erosion of purchasing power. The result was a COLA — not the kind that fizzes in a glass. This was a Cost of Living Adjustment. Soon unions and other wage earners clamored for their COLA.

It was all to no avail, however. Inflation seemed to move faster than the adjustments could be made. As President Carter gloomily put it, there was a malaise on the land.

Even the Federal Reserve seemed unable to control the growing inflationary threat. After Paul Volcker's appointment as Fed chairman, he changed the discount rate six times. The moves were dismissed as "insufficient" or, worse, "behind the curve."

With the 1980 presidential election looming, Volcker shifted to a policy to control the money supply. So Wall Streeters and the public were engaged in a Thursday afternoon ritual of "watching the Ms." Each Thursday, the Fed would release the data on the various forms of "money supply," from simple currency in circulation through money in mutual funds. Each had its own designation — M1; M2; M3, etc. The Thursday release was covered by more reporters than would follow Princess Di.

The reason for all the attention was the effect the policy was having (or not having) on interest rates. Rates climbed from 12 to 18 percent. By March of 1980, President Carter felt he had to act. He imposed credit controls which hit the economy like a sledgehammer. A major credit card company announced that it had lost a half-million cardholders. Sales of everything plummeted.

Interest rates bordered on the zany. Rates were at 20 percent when Carter made his move; plunged to 11 percent in July, when the economy had fallen of a cliff; and were above 21 percent by the end of 1980. But the end had already come for Jimmy Carter. Ronald Reagan had won the White House handily with the slogan "Are you better off today than you were four years ago?" As the vote indicated, most of America felt they were not better off.

Interest rates refused to cooperate with the new president. By June of 1981, the prime rate was still above 20 percent. Unfortunately, the unemployment rate in the manufacturing area also rose above 20 percent.

Nearly everyone blamed the Fed — and Volcker in particular. Editorial after editorial called him insensitive and out of touch. A man broke into Federal Reserve headquarters carrying a sawed-off shotgun. He was looking for Paul Volcker.

The economy continued to slip and sputter into the middle of 1982. Then a new worry arose. Mexico came to Washington to ask for help. Mexico was on the verge of defaulting on several hundred millions of dollars in debt. Most of that debt was owed to U.S. banks. Without relief, the banks might collapse like a house of cards.

By August of 1982, it was agreed. Mexico would get relief and the Fed would begin to ease — to allow more money into the system. The bond market began a dizzying rally. The stock market rallied 50 percent in less than half a year. It would turn out to be the start of the greatest and longest period of prosperity in American history. It would last even into a new millennium. There was just enough spice in the salsa, apparently.

There are certain events that freeze and focus the minds of whole generations. One certainly was the Kennedy assassination. An earlier one had been the stock market crash in 1929 and the follow-up of the Great Depression.

People's lifestyles were changed drastically. They told their children and their children's children of the awful consequences when a stock market tsunami hits.

So, in October 1987, when a new tsunami erased 25 percent of the value of the stock market, everyone froze — especially those who were at ground zero.

Ironically, while the press and history focus on Blue Monday, October 19, 1987, as that "awful day" when the Dow fell 508 points in astonishing volume, it was on the next day that America almost came apart.

But to understand that, you need to know a little bit about that awful Monday and how it happened. Actually, it had begun the week before.

Late in the day Friday, there had been rumors about the first lady's health and other rumors on the liquidity or indictability of some arbitrage brokerage firms. The fact that it was expiration Friday was also of little help. The Dow closed down 108 points.

The weekend brought little solace. The Japanese had imposed a 96 percent tax on real estate speculators. Could that bubble burst? Congressman Gephardt's trade deficit bill appeared to the ghost of Smoot, Hawley to gain support. The first lady went into Bethesda for cancer surgery. Germany changed its tax treatment on interest payments inhibiting the purchase of U.S. bonds. Treasury Secretary Baker, on national television, appeared to challenge Germany on their currency policy. He seemed to hint at a dollar in free-fall. And on Sunday there were predictions of a U.S. attack on Iran.

As traders arrived at the office early Monday, they were greeted by more reassuring news. Tokyo had fallen a record amount. Hong Kong was down 11 percent, London nearly 10 percent, Germany and the Netherlands around 8 percent and Paris nearly 12 percent. Foreign trading in the U.S. dollar and treasury bonds was in disarray. Rumors of weekend telephone redemptions in mutual funds ran to mind-bogging numbers.

At 8:30 a.m., newswires were alive with "informed sources" reporting of a U.S. military strike on Iran.

At 9:30, the New York Stock Exchange opened.

Prices began to fall from the get-go. In the first few minutes of trading, the S&P Futures had fallen more than they had in six hours of heavy selling Friday. In the first 90 minutes, the Dow was down 200 (over 10 percent). It tried to rally, but a misquote indicating that the SEC might halt trading spooked markets, and the Dow rolled over to close down 508 points (about a 25 percent drop in one day). One trader who loves numbers pointed out that the Dow had dropped 1 point every 47 seconds.

It was not a figure most of the floor would have computed. The volume of orders pouring onto the floor in a panic was unprecedented. For much of the day, over a 1,000 messages per second cascaded onto the floor. As one fellow put it, "traders and clerks looked like Lucy and Ethel boxing chocolates at a conveyor gone mad. Technology is great, but the machine doesn't have a wallet. Somebody's got to buy all this stuff."

Monday night, the lights burned long and late on Wall Street. But it was not just brokers up late. Government officials, agencies and banks — oh yes, banks — were sleepless.

Tuesday, many in Wall Street sensed the fabric of American finance was near to being irreparably torn. The problem was not technology, it was that good old standby — human nature.

This is the way some think it happened.

A few years before the crash, a big bank that was only a few yards from the New York Stock Exchange decided to expand its activity in brokerage lending. Its particular interest was in financing specialists positions. It even had a very knowledgeable person in charge. So over time, the number of specialist clients, the size and number of loans and the profits to the bank all grew handsomely.

Then, came Monday, October 19, 1987.

Electrified by the crash (and reminiscent of 1929), the bank chairman called the comptroller and said something like — "Bob, do we have any exposure in this stock sell-off?" After an hour or two to check, Bob reported that all the bank's blue chip clients appeared sound and the only direct relationship was the specialist financing unit. "How big is that, Bob?" he was probably asked. "Well, Sir, the specialist unit as a whole looks to be X billion dollars." "What did you say Bob? These phones made it sound like you said billions with a 'B.' I did, Sir! It is billions."

That was all the chairman needed. He called "Frank" who ran the specialist financing group and told him that he wanted to see each of the specialist clients, one at a time, on Tuesday. The purpose was to review each of their accounts and to tell them their credit lines were cut.

Frank probably gasped and told the chairman that he, Frank, had been doing this for 35 years, and that the chairman was misreading the data. The chairman probably allowed as how experience, knowledge and judgement were usually assets, but when it came to billions with a "B," the chairman would make all decisions.

So beginning early Tuesday morning, each specialist was called in and told that

his credit line was tapped out. Each protested that the data was false. The chairman said — "But you bought $X billion and you'll owe that when the contract is due." The reply was usually, "Yes, but I was able to sell 90 percent of the X billion (usually at a loss) but anyway that means I'm only liable for 10 percent of the amount you cite." "Oh yeah?" said the chairman. "How do we know the folks you sold to are good for the money? Sorry, no more credit."

Calls from the NYSE were unable to shake the chairman's mistaken conviction. The opening rally of Tuesday was quickly a memory, as those at ground zero thought the system might collapse. If credit lines to dealers were cut off, prices could go into total free-fall, cracking the financial system like an egg.

Luckily, a call to the Fed brought a call to the bank telling the chairman to reopen the credit lines. Word began to spread. Prices began to rally. More help came as companies announced buy-backs in their own stocks. The market rallied, and the system was saved. The quick action by the Fed gave Wall Street a respect and appreciation for Alan Greenspan that has lasted well over a decade. But as a Marine on Iwo Jima once said, "It was nice to be part of history, but I'd rather not do it again!"

THE OLD OAK AND BRASS TRADING POSTS WERE DISMANTLED
IN A 1980-81 RENOVATION. THIS ONE FOUND A NEW HOME
GUARDING THE ENTRANCE TO THE MAIN DINING ROOM.

For the three quarters of the Stock Exchange Luncheon Club's existence, it was surrounded by scores of competitors. They had names like the Lawyers Club, the Bankers Club, the Harbor View Club, the City-Midday Club, the Downtown Association and many more. The quality of service, food and surroundings in each was as high as at any five-star restaurant.

But over the last few decades, changes in tax laws, business hours, business customs and relocations have seen virtually all these fabled locales shut their doors. The Stock Exchange Luncheon Club is one of the last few high-quality dining clubs in New York.

It has not just survived; thankfully, it has even thrived. That is due in no small part to the exceptional group of men who managed and guided the Luncheon Club through such perilous times.

As background to this book, we approached the past presidents, officers and board members, hoping they might share some challenge or crisis they had to face. Instead, each and every one of them brushed off reminiscences of both trouble and triumph. Rather, they suggested, we should recount some of the special anecdotes that have become woven into the fabric of this century-old family.

So, in gratitude for their exceptional service, judgement and guidance, we will follow their collective wish. With names omitted to protect the innocent (and others) here follow a few recollections.

The Stock Exchange Luncheon Club has had a collection of exceptional Persian rugs in the clubhouse for decades. Over the years, the value of this group of rugs grew and grew. Each year, the club would arrange to have the rugs picked up in late spring, carefully cleaned and re-conditioned, stored and then returned in fall to their traditional places on the club floors.

One year, an impromptu summer audit by the House Committee seemed to turn up some inconsistencies in the books. A further review failed to resolve the issue, and one key employee changed his employment. The board tightened controls and moved on. No charges — just changes.

As Halloween approached, one of the House Committee members noticed the rugs were still not back on the floor. They inquired of the cleaner. The rugs, he told them, had been delivered to a rug dealer at the instructions of "someone" at the Luncheon Club. Calls to the "dealer" were not returned (since the dealer had gone out of business).

The board went into a dither. A valued asset was lost. Forget the value. An heirloom of the membership, entrusted to their stewardship, was gone. The rugs had to be replaced!

The search began. Decorators, rug merchants, importers, even manicurists — anyone and everyone was asked about rugs. No one knew of the availability of the right number, size and color needed. Then, as December neared, and with it the crisis of a rugless Club Christmas party, a decorator called to say that she had heard that an "estate collection" in a warehouse was comparable to the specifications.

A board delegation was dispatched, the comparability noted and the rugs were purchased. The delegation toasted their success — several times.

A week later, the new rugs were brought in and carefully arranged on the floors. A collective sigh of relief was heard. Then, one of the Luncheon Club employees implored a board member to follow him to see "something" on one of the rugs. Was it a cigarette burn, a wine stain, a fabric tear? When he arrived at the rug in question, the board member just stared, and then he burst out laughing. There, on the underside of the rug, was a label — "Property of Stock Exchange Luncheon Club." The titans of Wall Street had managed to buy back their own rugs. They still claim the price was fair.

THE TRUTH, THE WHOLE TRUTH
AND NOTHING BUT THE TRUTH

As the focus of the club began to expand to include floor deliveries, the House Committee noted that one of the most popular requests was the "chunk white meat chicken salad." At a board meeting, committee members asked the salad chef what kind of chicken he used to make the dish so popular.

The salad chef stammered for a moment and then revealed that virtually all the best restaurants in New York (and elsewhere) tend to make "chunk chicken breast" from turkey breast (something to do with the expected chunk size).

The board members were aghast. "You make chicken salad with turkey? No more! We tell the truth! Change the menu to reflect the truth. Have it read 'Turkey Salad.'" The change was made, and the effect was immediate. Instead of 200 orders per day of chicken salad that everyone raved about — the Luncheon Club now received five orders a day for turkey salad. Ironically, some surrounding takeout places reported a sudden surge in orders for chicken salad and asked if we could lend them some turkey breast to meet the new demand.

Truth in advertising sometimes has unexpected results.

TROPHY HEADS ADORN THE WALLS BY THE ELEVATORS.

The lobby of the Luncheon Club has long been renowned for the big game trophy heads mounted on the walls. Each was a hunting trophy bagged by a club member more than a half-century ago and donated to the club for display.

In the late 1960s, a friend of a member visited the club and was quite taken with the display. He himself was a hunter of great note and suggested to his friend that he would like to donate one of his trophies to the Luncheon Club collection. The member, who was on the board, conveyed the offer at a meeting.

The board may have been conducting a wine tasting at this particular meeting. There are few other explanations for why they accepted the offer. The hunting trophy in question was the head of an African elephant.

When the truck arrived, the crew quickly noted the elephant head could not fit through any door. After a rather comical attempt, it was demonstrated that it would not fit into the service elevator.

The friend of the donor began calling for a crane to hoist the head up to the seventh floor. Fortunately, someone pointed out that even with a crane, there was no window large enough for the trophy. That may be the reason that to this day there is no elephant head on the walls.

THE LUNCHEON CLUB READING ROOM.

Many charities like to use the ambiance and background of the Luncheon Club for dinners, raffle drawings or even promotion. A few decades back, a famous charity (whose innocence *will* be protected) promoted an event by commissioning and then displaying a very large painting, which was by a painter who was very, very well known, as was his style.

The painting was so large that it arrived as a rolled canvas, unframed. It was then mounted and framed and hung for display in the Luncheon Club's Reading Room. Furniture was moved to best display this (perhaps) 15' by 8' grand design.

One night, after about a week of display, the painting hung quietly in a deserted Luncheon Club at 8:00 p.m. on a Friday night. In the interest of truth, "deserted" may be an exaggeration. "Almost deserted" might be more correct.

Two members remained in the bar. Not wanting to keep the staff late, they had ordered more than their usual 19 rounds and squirreled the excess under the table. They then bid the staff a "happy weekend with the family" and remained to decant the hidden overage.

Then, enlightened more than the average mortal, they headed for home — or somewhere. As they passed the Reading Room, the more judicious of the two was struck by the beauty of the painting.

It would look perfect in his knotty pine basement rec room. No matter that the painting was larger than any wall in the rec room (or perhaps the house), Beauty is Beauty; Art is Art! The two began to remove the expensive painting from the Reading Room wall. Somehow, they managed to negotiate the painting up to the elevators. There they faced a geometry problem that would baffle even Euclid.

Luckily, members of the security team arrived before they had put a foot through the painting or tried to unframe it with a set of keys. The security folks convinced them that the painting might detract from the ambiance of the rec room, or at least clash with the aquarium. Martha Stewart could not have done better.

The charity raffle went well!

Each year the Luncheon Club puts out a series of holiday displays. One of the most extensive (and most commented upon) is the Christmas display. A key portion of this display is the "Dickens Village," a collection of ceramic figurines and houses laid out at the entrance of the Dining Room.

One day, a club staff manager walked by the "Village" and stopped suddenly. Something didn't seem quite right. After a careful review, he discovered that the "sleigh and team" were missing. Puzzled, he began to search about.

One of the Dining Room staff suggested that he had seen a certain club member pocket the figurines early that morning. The manager approached the club president with this "delicate" problem.

The next morning, the president approached the member in question and asked about the missing figurines. The member protested that he had thought they were simply toys and had given the sleigh and team to his little granddaughter. You couldn't expect him to break a little girl's heart and wreck her faith in her grandfather.

The president said he understood perfectly. He suggested an alternate solution. Simply replace the missing pieces. The "Village" set was no longer produced, but an antique dealer might have a sleigh and team for, perhaps, $3,000.

The next morning, the sleigh and team had somehow returned. Another Christmas miracle.

STOCK EXCHANGE MEMBERS HAVE ALWAYS ENJOYED CHRISTMAS.

I "Urned" A Place In This Place

Given recent market volatility and activity, it is small wonder that the Reading Room and the Game Room are not heavily populated at midday. In fact, they are usually deserted except for the rare member trying to sneak 40 winks in a 10-minute break.

That's just how lonely it was in the late 1980s, when the water turned to something other than wine.

At the time, in the Ante Room to the Bull and Bear Grill, members could always find a frosty pitcher or two of iced water and the necessary glasses. The pitchers were kept frosty cold whatever the season.

Apparently, on this particular day, one of the older members was shuffling toward the ice water. As he arrived at the table, he looked about and saw no one but a sleeping member in a wing chair (part of the 40-wink brigade). He removed his dentures and poured a half-glass of water. In the glass, he inserted the dentures and his finger. We can only surmise that he had recently received a new but ill-fitted set of dentures. He rubbed the cooled finger on his gums and re-inserted the cooled dentures.

Apparently, the caloric transfer was not satisfactory. He again took out the dentures and now swirled them several times in the ice-filled pitcher. After an adequate time to adjust several BTU's, he picked up the dentures and put them back in his mouth, apparently satisfactorily, and shuffled off.

Unbeknownst to Mr. Happy Tooth, his every move was being watched in shock by Mr. 40-Winks (who couldn't sleep now if you chloroformed him). He jumped from his seat and called for a waiter to empty and wash the water pitchers. He then ran to relate the tale to the club president.

The president was even more shocked. The water supply must not be violated. Luckily, he just happened to know a friend in the silver water-urn business and, for a mere $2,000, was able to get delivery in two days (plus $300 for a silver lock). Now water came from a locked urn with a spigot.

The board was so thrilled with this quick (but expensive) thinking that they voted to put the ashes of the president in the silver urn upon his demise. They were so enthusiastic about the price he had paid that they encouraged him to accept that honor as soon as possible.

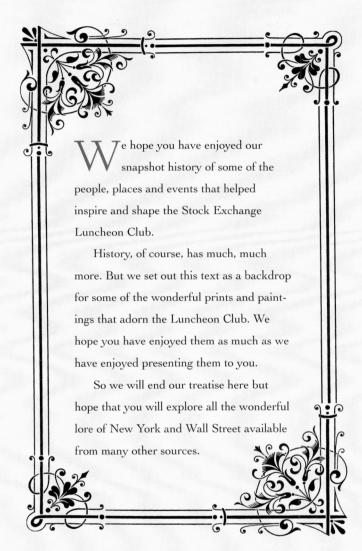

We hope you have enjoyed our snapshot history of some of the people, places and events that helped inspire and shape the Stock Exchange Luncheon Club.

History, of course, has much, much more. But we set out this text as a backdrop for some of the wonderful prints and paintings that adorn the Luncheon Club. We hope you have enjoyed them as much as we have enjoyed presenting them to you.

So we will end our treatise here but hope that you will explore all the wonderful lore of New York and Wall Street available from many other sources.

OFFICERS

John J. Dalessandro
President

Alfred O. Hayward, Jr.
Vice President

Robert J. Jacobson, Jr.
Secretary

Brian J. McNeary
Treasurer

Robert L. Cunningham
Assistant Secretary

William P. Weil
Assistant Treasurer

BOARD OF DIRECTORS

Arthur D. Cashin, Jr.

Peter C. Dully

John G. Leness

Terence S. Meehan

Christopher C. Quick

Joel M. Surnamer

GENERAL MANAGER

William E. Jessup